Creative Communicative Activities for the FRENCH Class

Linda Skaife

National Textbook Company
a division of *NTC Publishing Group* • Lincolnwood, Illinois USA

Acknowledgments

The author would like to thank those people in the West Valley-Mission Community College District whose support made this book possible, including Chancellor Gus Mellander, members of the Governing Board, and members of the Sabbatical Leave Committee. She would also like to gratefully acknowledge the longtime support and encouragement given by Edith Zanotti of West Valley College. A special thank you goes to Jackie Capurro of Mission College and Cathy Shapiro of NTC, for their suggestions and proofing, and to Manny Magallon, Sharon Hathaway and Dave Robison for their assistance with computer programs. Finally, a sincere thank you to Russell Nelson, artist and friend, whose graphics have greatly enhanced the final work.

The author and publisher wish to thank the following organizations and individuals for the use of the photographs on pages 167, 169, and 171: The American Institute of Certified Public Accountants; Karen Christoffersen; The Connecticut Culinary Institute; Delta College; Eastman Kodak Company; First Chicago Corporation; French Embassy Press and Information Service; Girl Scouts of the U.S.A.; Greenville Technical College; Hasbro, Inc.; Hawaii Visitors Bureau; The Institute for Paralegal Training; Betty McCasland; The National Restaurant Association; The Organization of American States; Catherine Shapiro; Bernard Turner; The United Brotherhood of Carpenters and Joiners of America; The University of Chicago Medical Center; Upjohn Healthcare Services; U.S. Department of Health and Human Services; U.S. Virgin Islands Department of Tourism; Walgreen Company.

1994 Printing

Published by National Textbook Company, a division of NTC Publishing Group.
© 1992 by NTC Publishing Group, 4255 West Touhy Avenue,
Lincolnwood (Chicago), Illinois 60646-1975 U.S.A.

Introduction

Foreign language teachers tend to be very creative. They meet the challenge of teaching students with wide ranges of ability and language level. They readily adapt to changing trends in language teaching and are eager to implement new teaching techniques and methodologies. However, most foreign language teachers face a serious obstacle to their creativity, namely time. Large numbers of students, increasing class loads, teaching assignments which often cover more than one subject area, professional responsibilities outside the classroom, all these things add up to very little time for the development of new ideas or the creation of new materials. Additional time pressures arise when large amounts of material must be covered each semester, leaving very little time for additional activities, or for the "fun stuff." The teacher is often faced with having to decide what to eliminate, especially if extra activities or projects are included.

The purpose of *Creative Communicative Activities for the French Class* is to help alleviate this situation. This book contains a variety of communication-based activities which are ready to use now. Teachers will find fully developed activities, complete with black-line masters for student handouts, teacher checklists, useful vocabulary, etc. The activities are lively and fun and they are effective teaching tools. They reinforce vocabulary and structures which would normally be studied so that the teacher is not faced with having to eliminate material in order to use them. The activities can be implemented at a variety of class levels and they are adaptable so that teachers can easily add their own special touches. In addition, the handouts contain a variety of graphic illustrations which aid comprehension and stimulate student interest. The result is an enjoyable and creative classroom atmosphere for the student and teacher alike, with a minimum of preparation time on the part of the teacher.

All activities included in *Creative Communicative Activities for the French Class* have been created with the following goals in mind: to facilitate communication and enhance oral expression, to stimulate student interest and enthusiasm, and to reinforce specific grammatical structures and vocabulary or cultural topics. While some activities are culturally specific, most can be adapted for use in other foreign language classes. Two of the activities are card games which call for specific responses on the part of the student and, as such, are not communication activities in the truest sense. They are included because, while reinforcing important grammatical concepts, they also help create a social, non-stressful atmosphere which encourages conversation and communication.

The activities have been cross-referenced by topic so that the teacher can readily see where an activity might fit in with the current unit of study. The activities can also be used independently of a lesson. It is suggested that handouts be prepared in advance and kept on file so that some of the more general activities can be pulled out on short notice for those times when a change of pace is necessary. As the teacher becomes familiar with each activity he or she will find new ways of using it. It is hoped that the activities in this book will be valuable teaching tools and that they will provide an enjoyable and effective means for stimulating communication in the French classroom.

CONTENTS

Activities by Topic

While each of the activities included in this collection uses a variety of language skills, some activities emphasize specific topics, grammatical concepts or vocabulary. These have been cross-referenced here so that they may be easily located for related lessons.

QUELLE COÏNCIDENCE

A Communication Activity

Objectives:	*To provide conversational practice and promote effective communication *To reinforce the use of interrogative expressions
Level:	Advanced beginning and intermediate
Number of students:	Entire class or large group
Materials:	One copy of *Quelle coïncidence* handout per student
Directions:	*Using only French, students circulate within the class asking questions of other students to find someone with whom they have the item listed in common. The name of one student for each item is then written in the blank under that item. *At the end of whatever time limit has been set, or when the first student has successfully completed the activity, the student(s) with the most answers can be asked to identify each of the students on his or her list. The answers can be verified with the class. *Additional questions can then be asked of other students in the class. Answers given in complete sentences further reinforce vocabulary and sentence construction.
Note:	The activity works best if the instructor first goes over any words which may not be familiar to students and then reviews the use of interrogative expressions with the class. A list of interrogative expressions likely to be used in the activity is given below.

Useful Vocabulary:

Quel(le) est...   *les genres de film:*
Qui est...   *un western*
Combien de...   *un film d'aventure*
De quelle couleur...   *un film policier*
En quel mois...   *une comédie (musicale)*
Quel âge avez-vous (as-tu)? *un film de science fiction*
                             un film d'épouvante

QUELLE COÏNCIDENCE!

Ecrivez le nom d'un(e) étudiant(e) qui a quelque chose en commun avec vous (le même nombre de personnes dans la famille, la même marque de voiture, etc.).

C'EST VRAI? #I

A Communication Activity

Objectives: *To enhance communication skills
                         *To stimulate critical and creative thinking
                         *To enrich vocabulary

Level: Advanced beginning, intermediate or advanced

Number of students: Entire class, divided into groups of three

Materials: One card from the *C'est vrai?* handout sheet for each group of
                         three students

Directions: *Cut the handout sheets into separate cards. (There are two pages of
                         cards for each level. Level 1 is intended for advanced beginning
                         students; definitions on the cards are given in English. Level 2 is
                         for intermediate and advanced students; definitions are in French.)
                 *Each card contains a word which is most likely unfamiliar to the
                         class. The teacher can choose which card each group receives or
                         (after eliminating any words a particular class might know) can
                         have one student from each group draw a card at random.
                 *Each group has seven to eight minutes to invent two new
                         definitions for its word and to prepare a sentence which
                         illustrates each meaning. The object is to make the false
                         definitions so convincing that they fool the rest of the class.
                 *Each of the three students from the group then defines the word
                         in front of the class and gives an example of its use in a sentence.
                 *Class members then vote for the student they believe is telling
                         the truth. The tally is recorded and the true definition is revealed.
                         The group scores one point for each incorrect guess.
                 *This continues until all groups have presented their definitions.
                         The group with the most points (e.g. incorrect guesses) wins.

Note: The activity works best if the instructor first models the exercise,
                         writing a word on the board and then offering three definitions,
                         illustrating each with a sentence. The students can then try to
                         guess which definition is the correct one.

C'est vrai?

une dragée

sugar-coated almond traditionally served at weddings and baptisms

i.e. Les enfants adorent manger les dragées.

fat

conceited, smug

i.e. L'homme était très beau mais il était aussi arrogant et fat.

un prestidigitateur

a magician

i.e. Houdini était un prestidigitateur dont la spécialité était l'évasion.

bigarré

many colored, gaily colored

i.e. Le touriste portait une chemise curieusement bigarrée.

un démêloir

a long-toothed comb

i.e. Un démêloir sert à démêler (untangle) les cheveux.

vétuste

dilapidated, old and timeworn

i.e. Dans le champs il y avait une petite maison vétuste.

randonnée

outing, excursion

i.e. Nous sommes allés faire une randonnée à pied en Bretagne

farouche

shy, timid, unsociable

i.e. Le chat était un peu farouche; il s'est réfugié derrière le divan quand l'enfant est entré dans le salon.

C'est vrai?

un périple

a voyage, journey or tour taken by land or sea

i.e. Ils on fait un périple en Grèce pendant les grandes vacances.

tergiverser

procrastinate, hem and haw

i.e. Il n'aime pas prendre des décisions; il a tendence à tergiverser.

furibond

furious, livid, hopping mad

i.e. Elle va être furibonde en apprenant la nouvelle.

la xénophobie

fear or hatred of strangers or foreigners

i.e. Le nationalisme peut s'accompagner parfois de la xénophobie.

un exutoire

an outlet or release

i.e. Il faut trouver un exutoire à sa colère; sinon il risque de tomber malade.

brimer

to aggravate or bully

i.e. Le petit tyran brimait sans arrêt son petit frère.

une culbute

a somersault

i.e. Les enfants jouent parfois à faire des culbutes sur la pelouse.

blafard

pale, pallid, wan

i.e. Son visage blafard reflétait sa mauvaise santé.

C'est vrai?

une dragée

une amande recouverte de sucre durci
(Les dragées sont traditionnellement offertes
à l'occasion de baptêmes et de mariages.)

i.e. Les enfants adorent manger les dragées.

fat

vaniteux, infatué de soi-même, (trop) content de
soi-même

i.e. L'homme était très beau mais il était aussi
arrogant et fat.

un prestidigitateur

un magicien

i.e. Houdini était un prestidigitateur dont
la spécialité était l'évasion.

bigarré

formé de couleurs ou de dessins variés

i.e. Le touriste portait une chemise curieusement
bigarrée.

un démêloir

un peigne à dents écartées (long-toothed)

i.e. Un démêloir sert à démêler (untangle)
les cheveux.

vétuste

vieux et détérioré par le temps

i.e. Dans le champs il y avait une petite maison
vétuste.

randonnée

une excursion, une longue promenade avec
plusieurs arrêts

i.e. Nous sommes allés faire une randonné à
pied en Bretagne.

farouche

timide, réservé, peureux, insociable

i.e. Le chat était un peu farouche; il s'est réfugié
derrière le divan quand l'enfant est entré dans le
salon.

11

C'est vrai?

un périple

un voyage touristique par mer ou par terre

i.e. Ils on fait un périple en Grèce pendant les grandes vacances.

tergiverser

retarder une décision par faiblesse ou par mauvaise volonté

i.e. Il n'aime pas prendre des décisions; il a tendence à tergiverser.

furibond

furieux, pris d'une violente colère

i.e. Elle va être furibonde en apprenant la nouvelle.

la xénophobie

l'hostilité à l'égard des étrangers

i.e. Le nationalisme peut s'accompagner parfois de la xénophobie.

un exutoire

un moyen de se débarasser d'une difficulté ou de ce qui gêne

i.e. Il faut trouver un exutoire à sa colère; sinon il risque de tomber malade.

brimer

soumettre à des vexations, contrarier

i.e. Le petit tyran brimait sans arrêt son petit frère.

une culbute

l'action physique qu'on fait en mettant la tête et les mains par terre et en roulant sur le dos, les pieds passant au-dessus de la tête

i.e. Les enfants jouent parfois à faire des culbutes sur la pelouse.

blafard

pâle, terne

i.e. Son visage blafard reflétait sa mauvaise santé.

C'EST VRAI? #2

A Communication Activity

Objectives: *To enhance communication skills
                   *To stimulate critical and creative thinking

Level: Advanced beginning, intermediate or advanced

Number of students: Entire class, divided into groups of three

Materials: No materials needed

Directions: *Each student in the group chooses an interesting experience he or
                   she has had and relates it to the others in the group. Twelve to
                   fifteen minutes are allowed for this part of the activity, four to
                   five minutes for each student.
                   *The groups are then given an additional twelve to fifteen minutes
                   to select one of the stories to relate to the class and to complete the
                   rest of the exercise. To do this, each member of the group prepares
                   his or her own version of the same experience. The student who
                   has had the actual experience must present an accurate version;
                   the other two may embellish it as they see fit.
                   *After the group has presented its versions, class members vote for
                   whichever student they believe is telling the truth. Each
                   incorrect vote scores one point for the group. When all groups
                   have completed their presentations, the group with the highest
                   score wins.

ACHETONS DE LA GLACE

A Communication and Role-Playing Activity

Objectives:
*To provide conversational practice and promote effective communication
*To reinforce the student's ability to use numbers in practical situations
*To familiarize the student with French money

Level:
Advanced beginning, intermediate or advanced

Number of students:
Any number of students, working in pairs

Materials:
One set of handouts for each pair of students
(Handout A should be copied onto silver or gray paper if possible and handout B onto tan or brown paper, as the silver-colored coins are arranged separately from the darker ones to give a more realistic feeling. If handouts A and B are laminated before giving to students to cut out, the coins and banknotes can be saved so that it is not necessary to duplicate these handouts each time the activity is done. The drawing of the ice cream vendor can also be reused.)

Directions:
*This activity should be used in conjunction with a lesson on French currency and coins. Prior to doing the activity in class, students can be asked to cut out the coins and banknotes and to bring them to class in an envelope marked A or B according to which handout they received. Only one copy of each handout is needed for each pair of students so each student only needs to cut out one page. Be sure, however, to distribute an equal number of both A and B. The first time you may wish to have a few extra copies prepared in case of absences.
*Ask students to divide up into pairs so that each pair has one envelope of money marked A and one marked B.
*As an introduction to the activity, the teacher may wish to use TPR techniques to familiarize students with the various denominations of coins and bills (only 20F and 50F notes are used in this activity): e.g. *Montrez-moi une pièce de dix francs. Prenez toutes les pièces de dix francs. Combien y en a-t-il? Mettez-les avec les pièces de deux francs. Quel est le total? Ajoutez deux pièces de vingt centimes...etc.*
*Distribute one copy of the drawing of the ice cream vendor with prices and one worksheet to each pair of students. Students follow directions on the *Achetons de la glace* worksheet, first completing the fill-in part of the exercise together and then acting out the role-playing situations.
*When the time allotted for the role-playing activities is over, the teacher should go over the written answers with the class.

Note:
For the teacher's convenience, answers to these exercises appear on the following page.

ACHETONS DE LA GLACE

ANSWERS TO EXERCISES

I. A. 1) 17F60   I. B. 1) 2F40

    2) 15F35   2) 0F65

    3) 22F80   3) 27F20

    4) 17F70   4) 1F30

    5) 34F95   5) 5F05

II. 184F55 (This is the total for coins and banknotes from handouts A and B; it will most likely be accurate only the first time the activity is done as coins tend to get lost with use. One way to reinforce both numbers and carefulness is to have students count the money aloud as they put it into their envelopes at the end of the activity.)

Parfum du mois

Ananas

CHOCO
CHOCO

PRIX DES GLACES

Parfums	Simple	Double
Vanille	6,30	8,70
Chocolat	6,40	8,80
Fraise	6,45	8,85
Abricot	6,55	8,95
Framboise	6,45	8,85
Pêche	6,85	9,25
Banane	7,60	9,50
Ananas	6,50	8,90
Pistache	6,50	8,90
Orange	6,55	8,95
Citron	7,60	9,50
Café	6,40	8,80

ACHETONS DE LA GLACE

I. Avec un partenaire, écrivez les réponses aux questions suivantes.
   A. Combien coûtent...
      1) deux glaces doubles au café?

      2) une glace double à l'orange et une glace simple
         au chocolat?

      3) trois glaces simples à la banane?

      4) deux glaces doubles à la fraise?

      5) une glace simple à la framboise et trois glaces doubles au citron?

   B. Si vous donnez les sommes suivantes au marchand pour chaque achat indiqué
   dans la partie I.A., combien d'argent vous rend-il?

      Pour #1, un billet de 20F...

      Pour #2, une pièce de 10F, une pièce de 5F, et une pièce de 1F...

      Pour #3, un billet de 50F...

      Pour #4, trois pièces de 5F et deux pièces de 2F...

      Pour #5, un billet de 20F et deux pièces de 10F...

II. Maintenant, sortez les billets et les pièces d'argent de l'envelope que vous avez et
rangez-les sur votre bureau entre vous et votre partenaire. Comptez l'argent. Combien
d'argent y a-t-il en tout?

III. Avec votre partentaire et l'argent que vous avez, jouez les rôles du marchand de
glace et d'un client qui voudrait acheter les glaces indiquées dans la partie I.A. Le
marchand ne doit pas oublier de compter la monnaie à haute voix. Quand vous aurez
fini, changez vos rôles et répétez l'exercice.

IV. Maintenant créez vos propres dialogues en achetant des glaces en quantités variées
avec votre argent et en rendant de la monnaie.

QUI SUIS-JE?

A Communication Activity

    Although varieties of this activity have been used by teachers for a long time, an attempt to make it easier to use by providing a ready-made list of identities is presented here. The first version contains a list of many of the well-known people who have made significant contributions to French culture. The second version is more general and does not require the same comprehensive cultural knowledge.

Objectives:	*To develop communication skills and to provide a lively opportunity for conversational practice *To reinforce skills necessary for obtaining information *To promote (French) cultural literacy (Version 1)
Level:	Intermediate or advanced (Version 1) Beginning (Version 2)
Number of students:	Entire class or large group
Materials:	One name label for each student
Directions:	*Separate the name labels on the following pages. If the labels are first laminated and then separated, they may be used with cellophane tape. This tape can then easily be removed so that the same labels can be used again in other classes. *Attach one name to the back of each student, without allowing the student to see it. *Students then circulate freely in the class asking questions of the other students in order to try and identify the person they represent. Only yes/no questions may be asked; information questions are not allowed. Examples should be given prior to beginning the activity such as: *Est-ce que je suis un homme? Est-ce que je suis vivant(e)? Est-ce que je suis acteur, un homme politique, un personnage historique, etc.* *When a student guesses his or her name correctly, the label is removed and given to the teacher and the student continues to participate by answering other students' questions. This continues until all the students have correctly guessed the name on their label. *If, after a reasonable amount of time, one or two students are not able to guess their own identities, the teacher might wish to change the game by allowing them to stand in front of the class while students help by giving them clues (e.g. *Vous avez vécu au XIXe siècle.*).
Notes:	*Versions 1 and 2 contain very different types of names. Version 1 is intended for use in a class where various aspects of French culture have been studied and the students have a certain degree of cultural literacy. If cultural literacy is a goal of the course, the activity could be used in conjunction with a written assignment in which students are asked to briefly identify a given number of people who have made contributions to French culture (when they lived, what field they were in, what their contributions were, etc.). This list would contain all the names from the *Qui suis-je?*

activity as well as other names from specific topics to be covered that semester (history, contemporary culture, art, Francophone countries, for example). Blank labels have been included so that the activity can be easily adapted to specific class interests. It is suggested that this assignment be given early in the semester with the understanding that at a later date, the class will be tested on it. *Qui suis-je?* can then be used as one of the review tools prior to the test.

*Version 2 requires only minimal cultural knowledge and so can be used by students with little awareness of French culture. An attempt has been made to limit names to only those well known in history or in contemporary popular culture so that students whose native culture is not American can participate fully. The teacher can further match names to individual student experience. As there are the names of "things" as well as people in this version, students should be made aware of this before beginning. This activity tends to be a very lively one, especially when a student guesses he or she is a *chien*.

*Additions to the blank labels could include the name of the teacher, the name of the school and the name of one or more students in the class.

Edith Piaf	Toulouse-Lautrec	Paul Gaugin
François Mitterrand	Louis Pasteur	Jean-Paul Sartre
Coco Chanel	Marguerite Yourcenar	Charlemagne
Napoléon Bonaparte	Louis Braille	Jeanne d'Arc
François Ier	Marie Curie	Jacques Cartier
Catherine de Médici	Claude Monet	Auguste Renoir
Molière	Auguste Rodin	Louis XVI
Victor Hugo	Claude Debussy	Marie Antoinette
Jacques Prévert	Charles de Gaulle	Frédéric Chopin
Jean de la Fontaine	Catherine Deneuve	Louis XIV

Dolly Parton	Michael Jordan	Joe Montana
Michael Jackson	le Président Bush	Whoopi Goldberg
la Tour Eiffel	Charles de Gaulle	George Washington
Napoléon Bonaparte	le Père Noël	Paul Newman
Martin Luther King, Jr.	François Mitterrand	Jane Fonda
la Maison Blanche	l'Arc de Triomphe	Tom Cruise
Marie Antoinette	Mme (Barbara) Bush	Mikhail Gorbachev
Garfield	la Princesse Diane	César Chávez
la Cathédrale de Notre Dame	Ronald Reagan	Johnny Carson
Snoopy	la Statue de la Liberté	Charlie Brown

QUI SUIS-JE?

LES EXTRATERRESTRES

A Communication Activity

Objectives: *To provide a lively opportunity for conversational practice and to promote effective communication
*To reinforce vocabulary associated with body parts, shapes and description

Level: Intermediate or advanced

Number of students: Any number of students, in groups of three

Materials: One set of *Les extraterrestres* drawings per class

Directions: *Separate the *extraterrestres* drawings; laminate if possible for future use.
*Review appropriate vocabulary with students. This would include words for body parts as well as a variety of descriptive adjectives. Students may be asked to "brainstorm," listing as many physically descriptive adjectives as possible. Lists will be different in each class depending on the level of acquired vocabulary.
*Divide students into groups of three. Have them decide which one will serve as an artist.
*Students are then presented the following scenario:

> Imagine that you and your partner are out for a pleasant evening stroll. All of a sudden, you see a strange, large, glowing object which appears to be some kind of flying saucer. It descends slowly and lands not far from where you are standing. And then...out of the space ship comes a live--and very unusual--form of being...a true *extraterrestre* ! It begins to approach you but suddenly turns and quickly heads back to the spaceship. As the spaceship ascends, its glowing lights disappear into the darkness.
>
> Now imagine that you must describe this *extraterrestre* to the police.

*The two students in each group who are not designated as the artist are given ten seconds to look at their *extraterrestre*. Each group is shown a different drawing; if there are more than 36 students in a class, two groups can work from the same drawing. In smaller classes, students may work in pairs with only one acting as observer.
*The observers then describe what they have seen to the "police artist" who composes a drawing according to their description.
*At the end of the time allotted, the teacher collects the drawings and, after showing each one to the class, displays the "originals." The comparison is sure to evoke laughter.

LES EXTRATERRESTRES

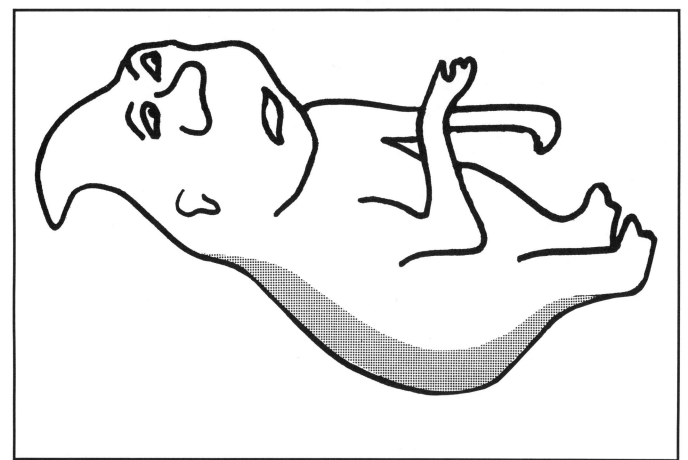

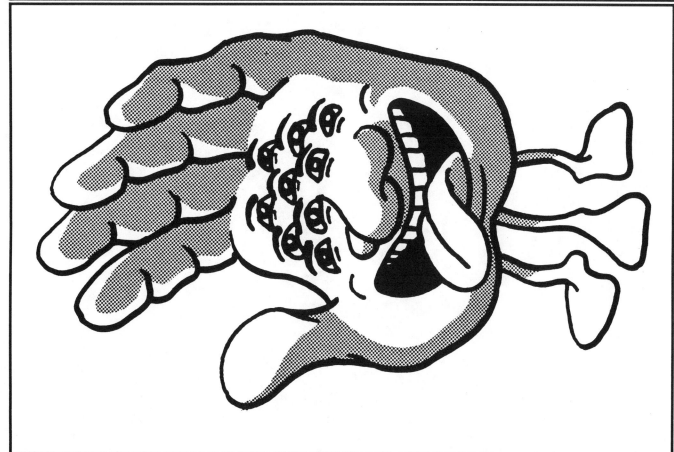

LES EXTRATERRESTRES

LES EXTRATERRESTRES

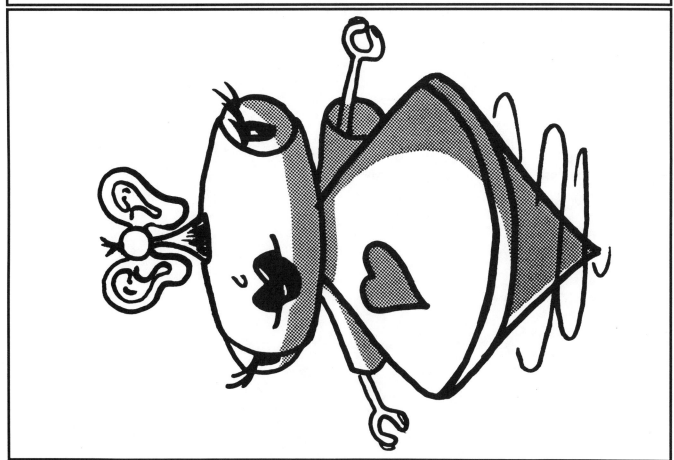

LES EXTRATERRESTRES

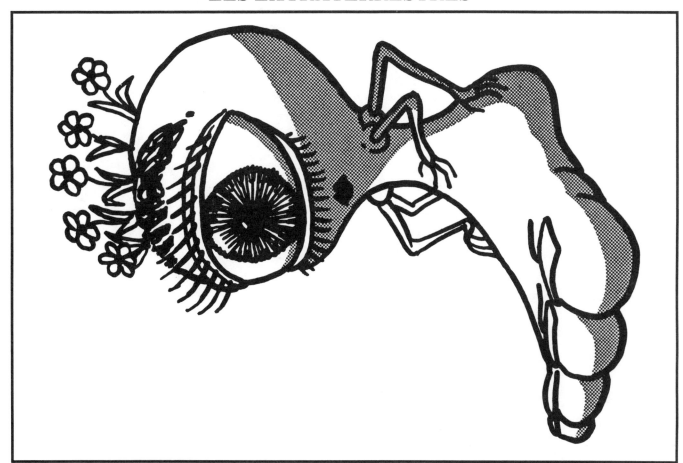

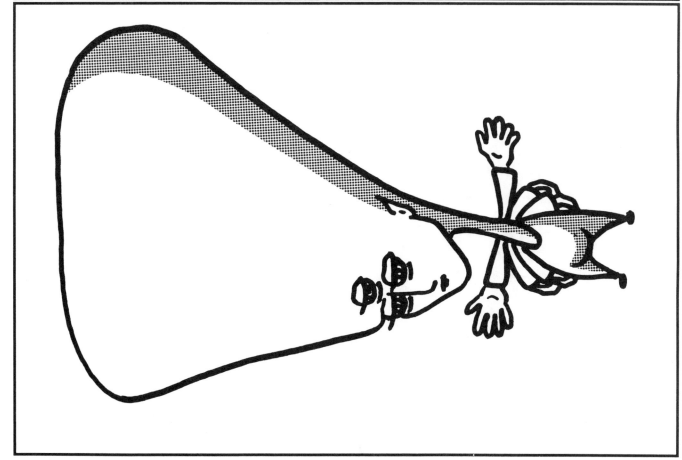

LES EXTRATERRESTRES

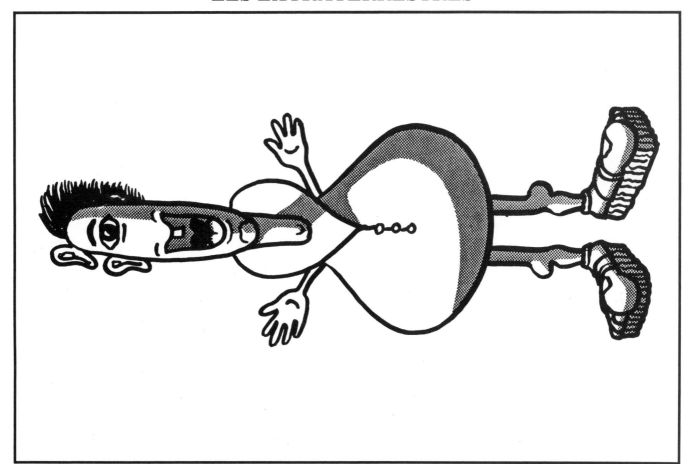

LES EXTRATERRESTRES

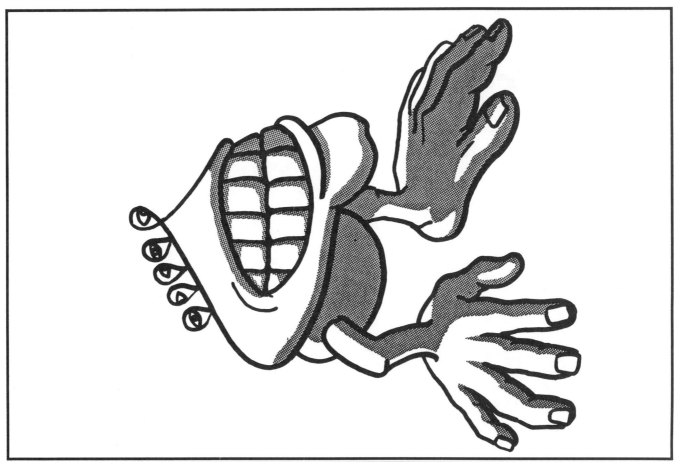

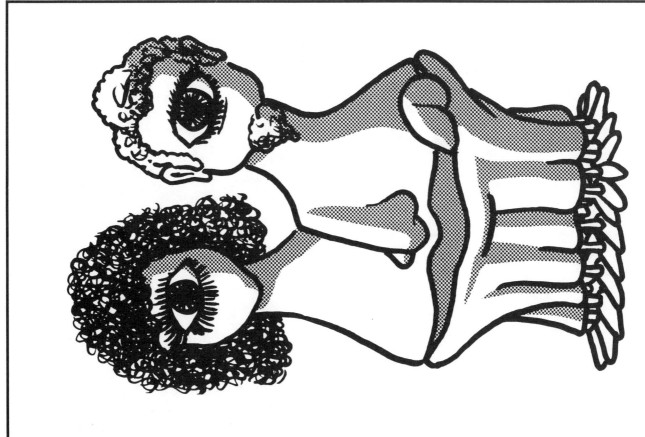

UN EFFORT COOPÉRATIF

An Oral Communication and Writing Activity

This is a very simple exercise which can be used early in beginning classes to reinforce basic writing skills or can be adapted to more advanced classes by lengthening the written exercise and discussion time accordingly. It reinforces both written and oral skills and, at the same time, helps to develop a sense of camaraderie and shared responsibility among students.

Objectives:
*To provide a task-oriented opportunity for effective communication
*To encourage students to work together cooperatively
*To improve writing skills
*To reinforce selected grammatical structures and/or vocabulary

Level:
May be adapted to all levels

Number of students:
Groups of four to six

Materials:
One copy of written worksheets for each group
Worksheets for levels 1 and 2 can be found on the following pages. More advanced students, working in smaller groups, could be asked to write a full page.

Directions:
*Students are assigned a topic or given a choice of topics relevant to the grammatical structures and/or vocabulary currently being studied. For example, students studying the *passé composé* might choose from among *Ce que j'ai fait hier soir (le weekend passé, l'été dernier), Mon premier jour à l'école, La première fois que je suis sorti(e) avec un garçon (une fille),* etc. Each student then develops one of the topics in writing. This may be done at home or in class. Beginning students are asked to write a paragraph, more advanced students up to a page. Anything longer becomes difficult to work with in a group activity. It is best to specify the length of the written assignment so that the results are fairly uniform.
*Once the students have checked their own work for errors, they are put into groups where, using only French, they must work together to correct each other's errors, discussing and explaining when changes need to be made. Within a given time period, depending on the size of the groups and the level of the students, students must reach a consensus on the final version of each written segment.
* Students then copy their own (corrected) work onto the worksheet provided and hand it in to the teacher. It is explained ahead of time that one grade will be given to the entire group for the final written product. The teacher may also wish to grade the oral part of the exercise for participation, effort, etc.

Notes: *This works very well in beginning classes where even students
          with very limited vocabularies can succeed in communicating
          basic concepts. At the same time it can help reinforce parts of
          speech. (The teacher may want to review some terms beforehand,
          such as: *nom, sujet, verbe, singulier, pluriel,* etc.)
          *As an added incentive, the teacher may wish to use topics from
          which test questions will be chosen for the chapter or unit test.

UN EFFORT COOPÉRATIF

Note pour
le projet _____

Groupe # _____
Etudiants dans le groupe: _____   _____

_____   _____

_____   _____

UN EFFORT COOPÉRATIF

Note pour
le projet _____

Groupe # _____
Etudiants dans le groupe:

_____   _____

_____   _____

_____   _____

_____

_____

_____

_____

_____

_____

_____

_____

_____

_____

_____

_____

_____

_____

_____

_____

_____

_____

_____

_____

OÙ EST SITUÉ...?

A Communication Activity

This activity can be used at a very early level as it does not require the use of verbs (other than the third person singular of *être*) and the only essential vocabulary, that of directions, can be easily learned as the activity is presented. It has the added benefit for beginning classes of reinforcing the use of the French alphabet.

Objectives:	*To provide conversational practice and reinforce communication skills *To familiarize the student with the geographical regions of France *To reinforce vocabulary associated with directions, location and geography
Level:	Novice, beginning and intermediate
Number of students:	Any number, divided into groups of two
Materials:	One copy of maps A and B for each pair of students
Directions:	*If students are not already aware of the significance of regional groupings or of their historical context, some discussion should take place concerning the *anciennes provinces* and the administrative divisions of *commune, département* and *région.* *Each pair of students is given two maps; one works from the first (complete) map (A); the other uses the second, incomplete one (B). Students may not see each other's papers. *The object is for students with the second map to fill in their maps with the correctly spelled names of the missing geographic regions. To do so, the first student gives locations (in reference to whatever places the two discover their maps have in common) and the second student confirms the locations and spelling by asking clarifying questions. *At the end of a given time period, or when the first pair has successfully completed the activity, the students compare maps and count the number of correct answers. The teacher can further review the activity by asking different students to respond to questions based on the completed maps.
Note:	In addition to modeling the activity with sample questions, the teacher may wish to first write the names of the regions on the board or an overhead transparency and have students repeat the names in order to reinforce correct pronunciation. The list should be erased, however, before the activity begins so that students must rely on each other for spelling.

Useful Vocabulary:

au nord de   *au sud de*
à l'est de   *à l'ouest de*
entre   *à côté de*
la côte   *la frontière*
Comment écrit-on...?

La France par régions

Où est situé...?

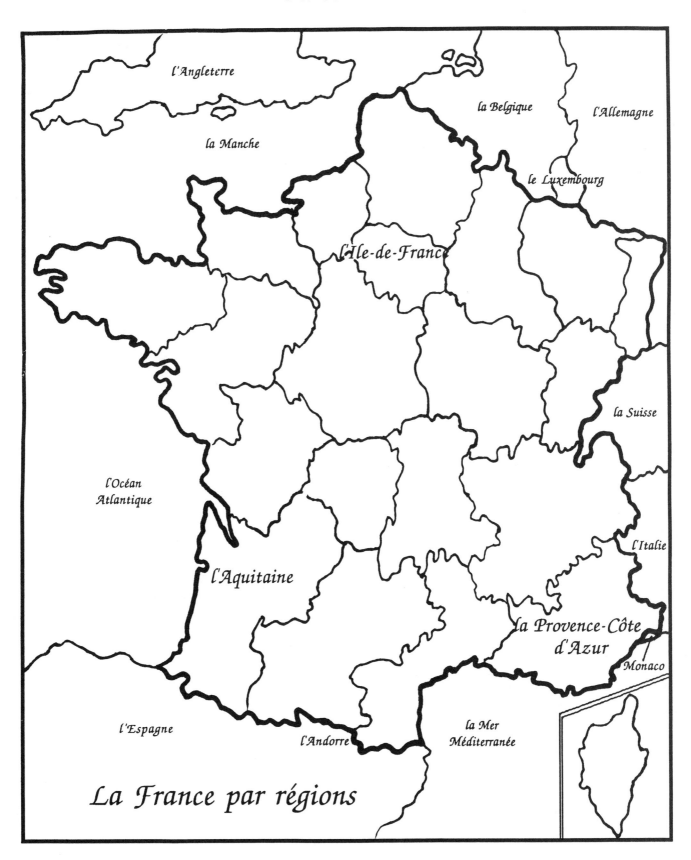

La France par régions

LA VINAIGRETTE

A Cooking Activity

This is a multifaceted activity which involves at least two class periods. It includes the introduction of specific vocabulary, a written translation exercise, a simple cooking demonstration by the teacher and a cooperative cooking activity on the part of the students. It requires quite a bit of prior preparation on the part of the teacher (mainly in the accumulation of cooking utensils, etc.) but proves well worth the effort in terms of enthusiasm generated, practical knowledge acquired and reinforced language skills.

Objectives:
*To provide a structured opportunity for conversation and communication in an enjoyable and nonthreatening atmosphere
*To enhance vocabulary, especially that associated with cooking
*To reinforce orally and in writing the use of the imperative
*To introduce students to an aspect of French cuisine and culture

Level:
All levels past novice

Number of students:
The class is divided into groups of three to six students each, depending on how many sets of cooking utensils are available

Materials:
*One copy of *La vinaigrette* handout for each student
*One copy of *Une recette pour la vinaigrette* for each student or an overhead transparency made from the handout
*One set of utensils and ingredients for each group (a detailed explanation and checklist are included on the following pages)

Directions:
*On the first day, vocabulary is introduced, the imperative is reviewed and the importance of *la salade* in everyday French cooking is explained. This provides an excellent opportunity for a discussion of the differences between French and American eating habits and cuisine.
*Students are asked to study the vocabulary and write a translation of the recipe as homework.
*During the following class period, the teacher reviews vocabulary and helps students correct their translations from the overhead transparency or recipe handouts.
*The teacher then gives a demonstration in French, using the appropriate vocabulary, of how to make *la vinaigrette*.
*Prior to the next step, the teacher may want to go over a few expressions not included in the lesson handout but which would be useful to the activity (e.g. *passez-moi s'il vous plaît, une presse à l'ail, des serviettes en papier, etc.*).
*Next, students divide into groups and, using only French, prepare the recipe and *une salade* collectively.
*If time permits, a *dégustation* can be held with a portion of each group's salad placed on a paper plate which has been numbered on the bottom according to its group. The order of the plates is then scrambled and all students (or a representative panel) sample the salad on each plate and then vote to see which one rates the highest.

*French bread, unsalted butter and something to drink (mineral water or bubbly cider work well) can be added and each group can then enjoy the remaining portion of its own salad.

Note: The *vous* form of the imperative has been used in this exercise to tie in with the structure usually introduced early in beginning classes. Thus the activity reinforces the use of this structure while providing a culturally oriented conversational activity which can be used by students who have studied very little French. If preferred, the imperative use of the infinitive, more commonly used in recipes, can be substituted.

Materials Checklist for *La vinaigrette*

For each group:

_____ 1 salad bowl
_____ 1 or 2 wooden spoons (for mixing and serving)
_____ tablespoon measure (or soupspoon)
_____ lettuce (one head lettuce for each 4-5 people)
_____ paper plates
_____ napkins
_____ plastic forks

For each two groups:

_____ vinegar
_____ oil
_____ salt
_____ pepper
_____ garlic cloves
_____ Dijon mustard
_____ garlic press
_____ 1/4 teaspoon measure
_____ paper towels for cleanup

If one set of ingredients is divided between two groups at two different work stations, (e.g. one garlic press for two groups, one bottle of oil, jar of mustard, etc.) it not only reduces the number of things to bring, but also increases conversation and participation as students go to neighboring tables to borrow items needed.

Optional:

_____ French bread (approximately one baguette for each 6-8 people)
_____ bread knife
_____ bread cutting board
_____ sweet butter (one cube for each baguette)
_____ plastic knives
_____ drinks (one liter bottle for each 5 people)
_____ paper cups

Notes: *Lettuce for a whole class can be washed and lightly dried the night before and stored in a clean pillowcase in the refrigerator. If the lettuce cannot be refrigerated until just before class, place two frozen blue ice containers, wrapped in newspapers, in the bottom of the pillowcase.
*Although the list of materials is long, one trip to a discount supply store for inexpensive stacking plastic salad bowls, disposable containers and paper products can simplify things. A discount import store is a good source for wooden spoons, garlic presses, tablespoon measures, etc. If stacking bowls are used, all nonperishables can be stored in a relatively small box for the next demonstration.
*The activity can be greatly simplified if students are divided into groups beforehand and each group is responsible for bringing its own ingredients and utensils.

LA VINAIGRETTE

Vocabulaire

Etudiez le vocabulaire suivant.

verbes:
1. mélanger	1. to mix
2. laver	2. to wash
3. sécher	3. to dry

noms:
1. la cuisine	1. a) cooking b) kitchen
2. un livre de cuisine	2. cookbook
3. une recette	3. recipe
4. le vinaigre	4. vinegar
5. la vinaigrette	5. traditional oil and vinegar "French" dressing
6. le jus de citron	6. lemon juice
7. l'huile	7. oil
8. une pincée	8. a pinch
9. le sel	9. salt
10. le poivre	10. pepper
11. une gousse d'ail (hachée)	11. (minced) clove of garlic
12. la moutarde	12. mustard
13. une cuillère à soupe	13. soupspoon, tablespoon
14. une cuillère à thé	14. teaspoon
15. une cuillère en bois	15. wooden spoon
16. la laitue	16. lettuce
17. la salade	17. salad (While this can mean a "composed" salad, it often is used to mean simply lettuce.)

Traduction

Traduisez la recette suivante en français.

A RECIPE FOR FRENCH DRESSING

Put in a bowl:
1 tablespoon of vinegar or lemon juice
3 tablespoons of oil
2-3 pinches of salt
1 pinch of pepper
1 clove of garlic, minced
1/4 teaspoon of Dijon mustard

Mix well with a wooden spoon.
Wash and dry the lettuce.
Put the lettuce in the bowl and mix well with the dressing.

UNE RECETTE POUR LA VINAIGRETTE

Mettez dans un bol:

    1 cuillère à soupe de vinaigre ou de jus de citron

    3 cuillères à soupe d'huile

    2-3 pincées de sel

    1 pincée de poivre

    1 gousse d'ail, hachée

    1/4 cuillère à thé de moutarde de Dijon

Mélangez bien avec une cuillère en bois.

Lavez et séchez la laitue.

Mettez la laitue dans le bol et mélangez bien avec la vinaigrette.

DES PENSÉES DIVERSES

A Communication Activity

Objectives:

*To provide conversational practice and promote effective communication
*To reinforce writing skills
*To help develop critical thinking skills

Level:

Advanced beginning, intermediate and advanced

Number of students:

Large groups or an entire class

Materials:

*One copy of fill-in sheet for each student (Two different versions, one for first year and one for more advanced levels, have been provided.)
*One blank form which will be used by the teacher to create handouts for the entire class (included in following pages)

Directions:

*The teacher writes the introductory phrases on the board and students are asked to complete each sentence by expressing their personal feelings and thoughts. This can be done either in class or as a homework assignment.
*The sentences are corrected and returned to the students who then copy them over (neatly, in black pen) on the form provided.
*The teacher then selects a number of responses, cuts them from the forms and attaches them to the blank form. Additional pages can be used if desired so that every student's work is represented. Copies are then made for each student.
*In class, students are given a specific length of time to identify the author of each *pensée* by circulating and asking questions of their classmates based on the information contained in their handouts.
*At the end of the time period, the class is surveyed to see how many originators of the *pensées* each student has identified and the teacher then completes the activity by asking questions of individual students to verify correct answers.

nom _____

classe _____

DES PENSÉES DIVERSES

Complétez les phrases suivantes en exprimant vos **véritables pensées.**

1. J'aime...

_____

2. Je n'aime pas...

_____

3. Les femmes...

_____

4. Le français...

_____

5. Souvent...

_____

6. Je voudrais...

_____

7. Notre professeur...

_____

DES PENSÉES DIVERSES

Complétez les phrases suivantes en exprimant vos **véritables** pensées.

1. J'aime...

2. Quelquefois je pense que...

3. Les femmes...

4. Je n'aime pas...

5. Les autres pensent que je suis...

6. Je voudrais...

7. Souvent...

8. La première chose que je remarque chez un homme (une femme) est...

9. Notre professeur...

10. Le moment le plus heureux de ma vie...

DES PENSÉES DIVERSES: Identifiez les étudiant(e)s qui ont exprimé les pensées suivantes.

nom

1) _____

2) _____

3) _____

4) _____

5) _____

6) _____

7) _____

8) _____

9) _____

10) _____

11) _____

12) _____

LA PUBLICITÉ

A Communication Activity

Objectives:	*To provide conversational practice and promote effective communication *To familiarize the student with useful vocabulary commonly found in restaurant advertisements (hours of operation, location, telephone numbers, etc.)
Level:	Advanced beginning, intermediate or advanced
Number of students:	Intended for pairs, may be adapted for two pairs of students working together
Materials:	One copy of handouts A and B for each pair
Directions:	*One student works from *publicité A*, the other from *publicité B*. Students may not see each other's papers. *The two handouts are similar but there are ten differences between the two versions. The object is for each pair to determine what the differences are within a given time period by asking questions in French. *At the end of the time period, or when the first pair has successfully completed the activity, the instructor reviews the differences in the two *publicités,* calling on students for answers.
Note:	The activity works best if the instructor first goes over any words with the class which may not be familiar to students. A partial list is included below. For the instructor's reference, an answer key to the activity has been provided following the student handouts.

Useful Vocabulary:

la publicité	*les huîtres*
ouvert	*les coquillages*
fermé	*accueil*
une dégustation	*antillais*
au choix	*T. L. J. (tous les jours)*

Restaurants

Restaurants

Restaurants

JEU DE POSSESSIONS

A Card Game

This game is not a true communication activity as it requires specific, structured responses from players. However, since the playing of a game in small groups provides an ideal opportunity for free conversation, it is included here in the hope that it will encourage authentic communication in a relaxed atmosphere, while at the same time reinforcing important basic grammar concepts.

Objectives:
*To help students differentiate between uses of the definite and indefinite articles
*To reinforce the formation of the possessive using *de* and the use of possessive adjectives
*To teach the vocabulary of common personal possessions

Level:
Beginning. May be used as a review early in an intermediate class.

Number of students:
Groups of three to five

Materials:
For each group: one set of forty cards. Print cards on heavy paper so that the drawings cannot be seen through the paper when held in the hand. Cards can be separated using a paper cutter; laminating them first increases their durability.

Directions:
*There are ten different "subjects" indicated in the upper left corner of each card. Each subject has four possessions which are indicated on the bottom. The object is to acquire as many sets of four as possible.
*The dealer shuffles the cards and distributes five cards to each player (six cards if there are only three in the group) and places the remaining cards in a pile in front of the players.
*The player to the left of the dealer begins by asking any student for a card he or she needs to complete a set of four. In order to do this, the player must have at least one card of that set in hand and must use the possessive construction with *de* in his or her question (e.g. *As-tu la brosse de Céline?*).
*If the student asked does not have the card, he or she responds in the negative but with a possessive adjective instead of the possessive construction with *de* (e.g. *Non, je n'ai pas sa brosse*). The player then draws a card from the pile and play passes to the student on the left.
*If the answer is affirmative, the student holding the card responds with: *Oui, voici sa brosse*, again using the possessive adjective, and gives the card to the player. The player continues asking for cards (of any of the students) until a negative answer is received and play passes to the student on the left.
*When a player has collected all four cards in a set, the cards are placed in a stack in front of the player. If a player runs out of cards he or she may draw from the pile during his or her turn as long as there are still cards in it. The game is over when all cards have been placed in sets. The student with the most sets wins.

Vocabulary:
In addition to reviewing the construction of the possessive and possessive adjectives, the instructor may wish to review the nouns used in *Jeu de possessions*. For this purpose, pages illustrating the vocabulary have been included which can be used to create overhead transparencies. The nouns used in this activity are also listed on the following page.

l'appareil-photo
la bicyclette
la brosse
la brosse à dents
le cahier
la calculatrice
le calendrier
la cassette
la chaîne-stéréo
le chat
le cheval
le chien
la clé
le crayon
le disque
la disquette
le gant de toilette
le journal
le livre
les lunettes

la machine à écrire
le magnétophone
le magnétoscope
la moto
l'ordinateur
la valise
la pâte dentifrice
le peigne
le poisson rouge
le portefeuille
la revue
le sac à dos
le savon
la serviette
la serviette de bain
le shampooing
le stylo
le téléviseur
la vidéocassette
la voiture

Notes:

*Nouns have been intentionally listed on the cards with indefinite articles so that students must switch to the definite article when using the possessive construction. Some nouns, however, are commonly named using the partitive (e.g. *du savon, de la pâte dentifrice*) and are consequently given in this construction. The teacher may wish to point this out.

Nous has been included as one of the subjects in order to show that the possessive with *de* is used with third person conjugations but not with the first or second persons. Students should be reminded that for this set only they will not use *de* in their questions but will use the possessive adjective in both question and answer (e.g. *As-tu notre calculatrice?*).

*The teacher may also wish to remind beginning students of the contractions of *de* and the definite article which will occur with some of the cards (e.g. *les crayons du professeur, le chien des enfants*).

nous

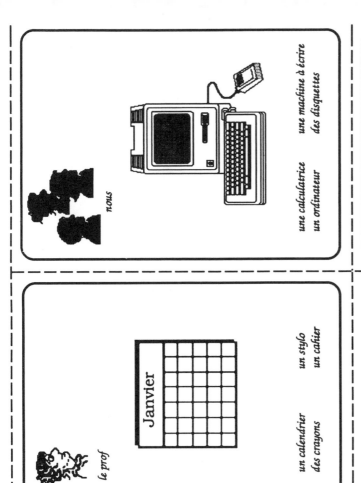

une calculatrice / un ordinateur
une machine à écrire / des disquettes

Gérard et Michel

une bicyclette / une voiture
une moto / des clés

le prof

un calendrier / des crayons
un stylo / un cahier

le bébé

du savon / du shampooing
un gant de toilette / de serviettes de bain

l'étudiant

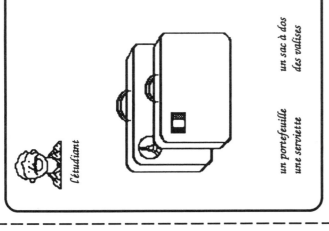

un portefeuille / une serviette
un sac à dos / des valises

les Tavernier

un magnétoscope / un téléviseur
des vidéocassettes / un appareil-photo

Céline

des revues / un livre
un journal / des lunettes

Vincent

des peignes / une brosse à dents
une brosse / de la pâte dentifrice

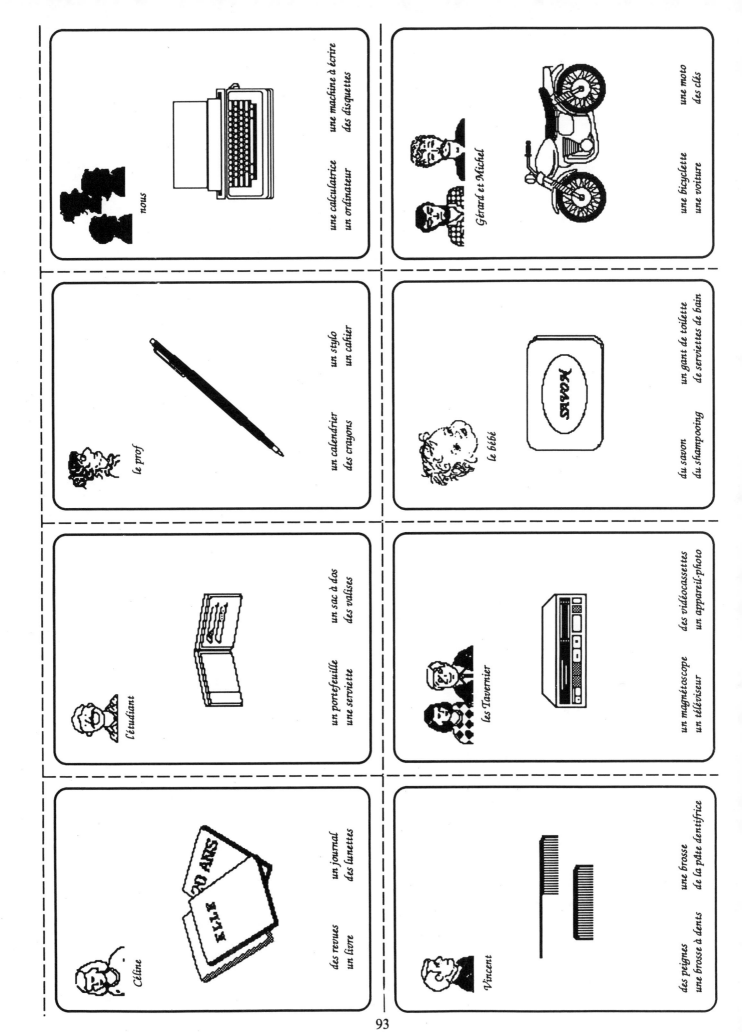

nous

une machine à écrire
des disquettes

une calculatrice
un ordinateur

Gérard et Michel

une moto
des clés

une bicyclette
une voiture

le prof

un stylo
un cahier

un calendrier
des crayons

le bébé

un gant de toilette
des serviettes de bain

du savon
du shampooing

l'étudiant

un sac à dos
des valises

un portefeuille
une serviette

les Tavernier

des vidéocassettes
un appareil-photo

un magnétoscope
un téléviseur

Céline

un journal
des lunettes

des revues
un livre

Vincent

une brosse
de la pâte dentifrice

des peignes
une brosse à dents

93

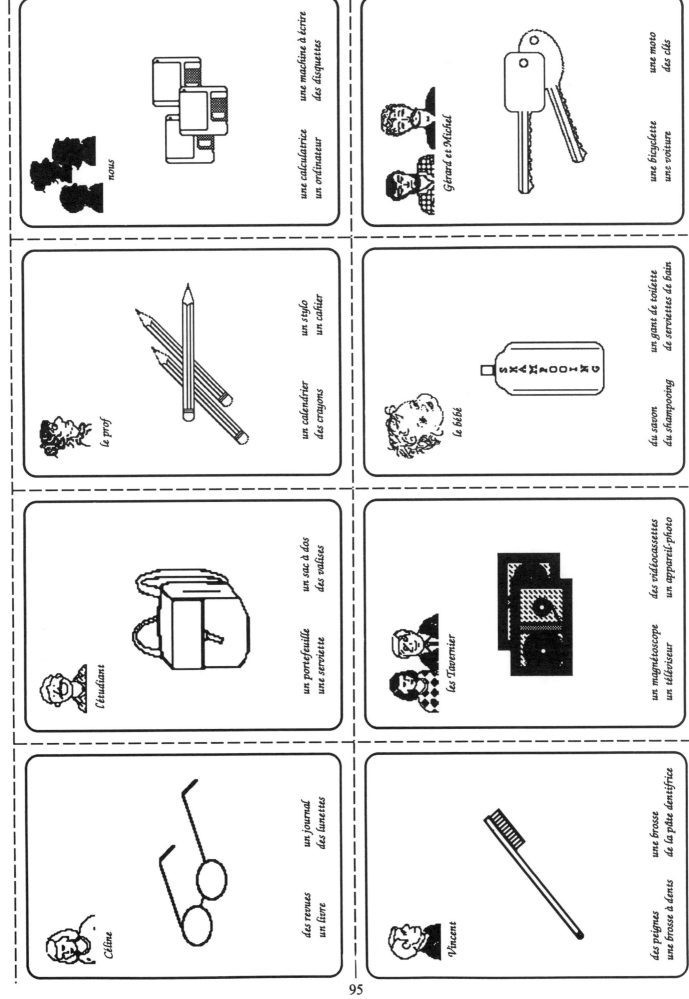

nous

une calculatrice   une machine à écrire
un ordinateur   des disquettes

Gérard et Michel

une bicyclette   une moto
une voiture   des clés

le prof

un calendrier   un stylo
des crayons   un cahier

le bébé

du savon   un gant de toilette
du shampooing   de serviettes de bain

l'étudiant

un portefeuille   un sac à dos
une serviette   des valises

les Tavernier

un magnétoscope   des vidéocassettes
un téléviseur   un appareil-photo

Céline

des revues   un journal
un livre   des lunettes

Vincent

des peignes   une brosse
une brosse à dents   de la pâte dentifrice

95

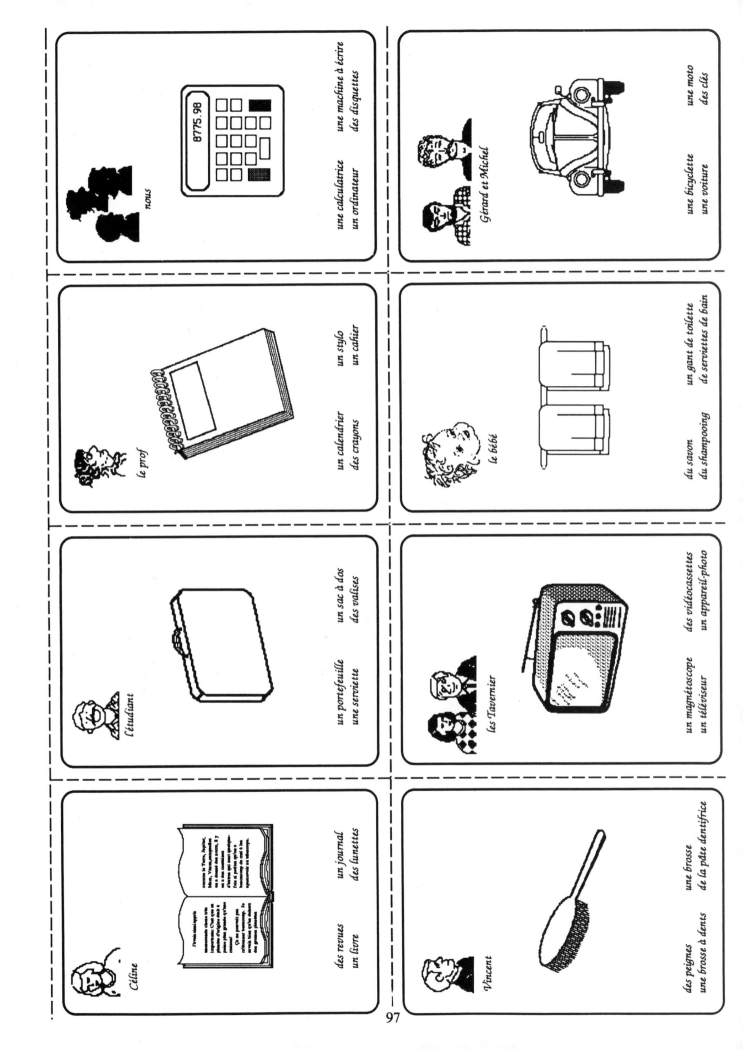

nous

une calculatrice — une machine à écrire
un ordinateur — des disquettes

Gérard et Michel

une bicyclette — une moto
une voiture — des clés

le prof

un calendrier — un stylo
des crayons — un cahier

le bébé

du savon — un gant de toilette
du shampooing — de serviettes de bain

l'étudiant

un portefeuille — un sac à dos
une serviette — des valises

les Tavernier

un magnétoscope — des vidéocassettes
un téléviseur — un appareil-photo

Céline

des revues — un journal
un livre — des lunettes

Vincent

des peignes — une brosse
une brosse à dents — de la pâte dentifrice

97

les enfants   un chien   des poissons rouges   un chat   un cheval

Monique et Suzanne   un magnétophone   une chaîne-stéréo   des cassettes   des disques

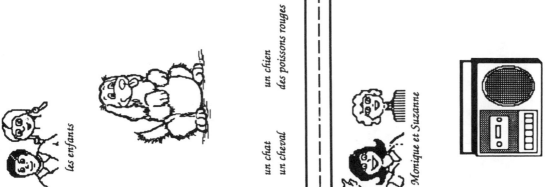

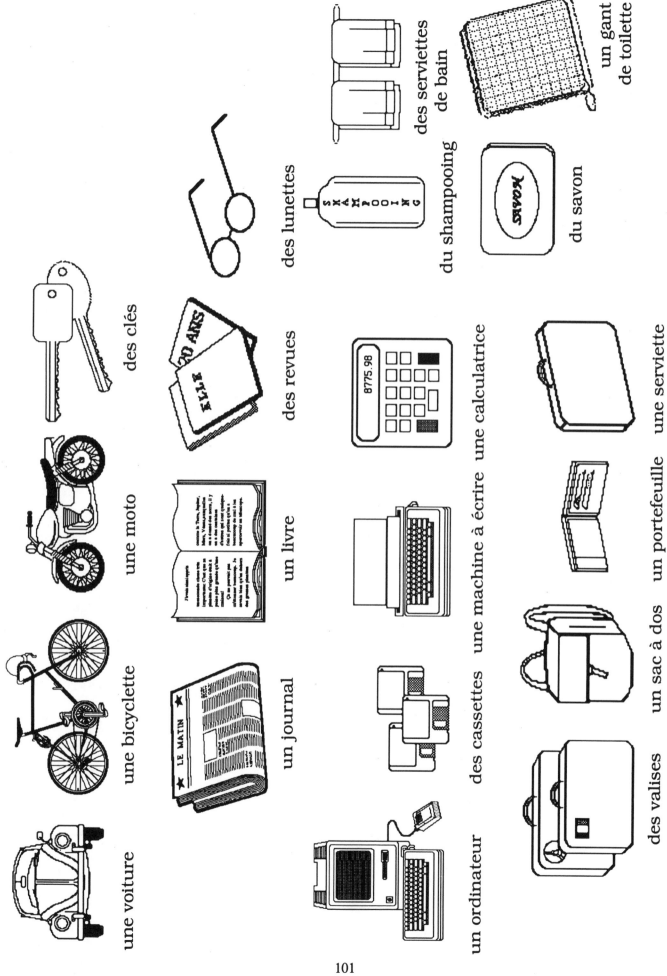

des clés

une moto

une bicyclette

une voiture

des revues

un livre

un journal

des lunettes

des serviettes de bain

un gant de toilette

du shampooing

du savon

8775.98

une calculatrice

une machine à écrire

des cassettes

un ordinateur

une serviette

un portefeuille

un sac à dos

des valises

LE MATIN

ELLE

SAVON

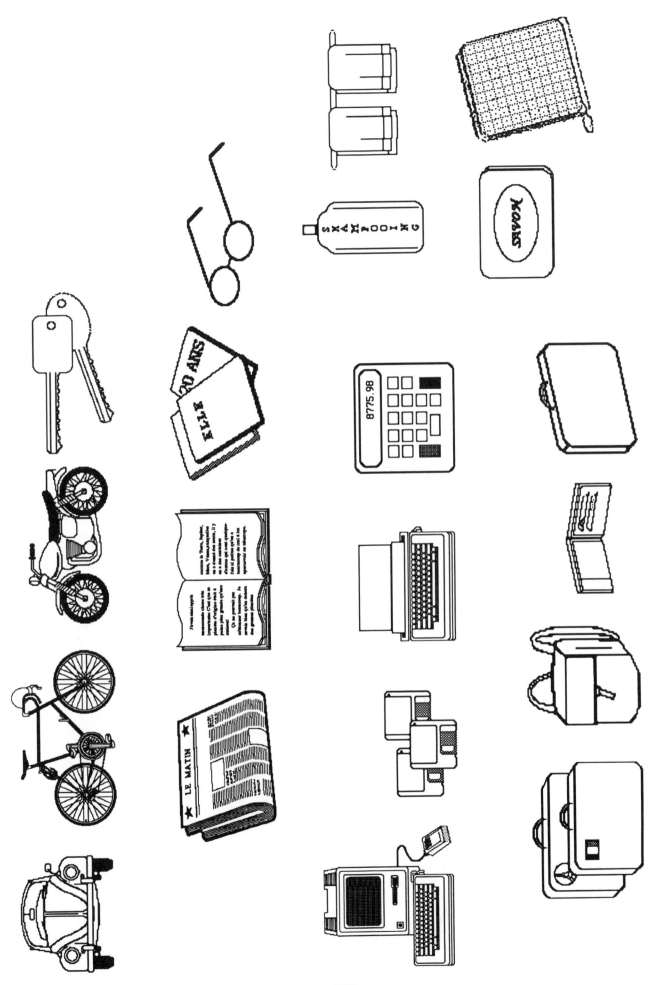

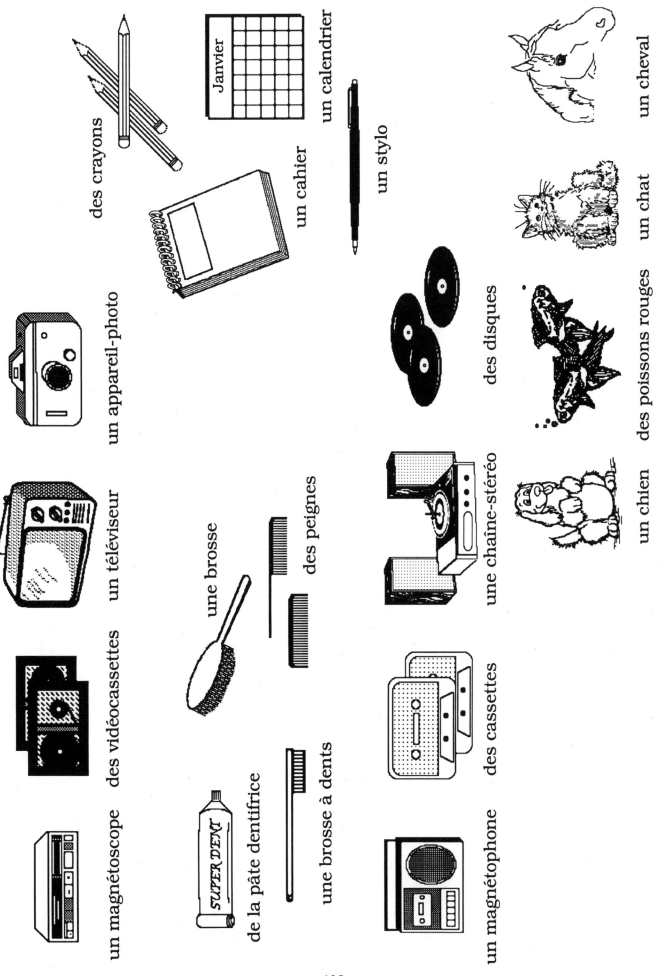

des crayons

un calendrier

un stylo

un cheval

un cahier

un chat

un appareil-photo

des disques

des poissons rouges

un téléviseur

des peignes

une brosse

une chaîne-stéréo

un chien

des vidéocassettes

une brosse à dents

des cassettes

un magnétoscope

de la pâte dentifrice

un magnétophone

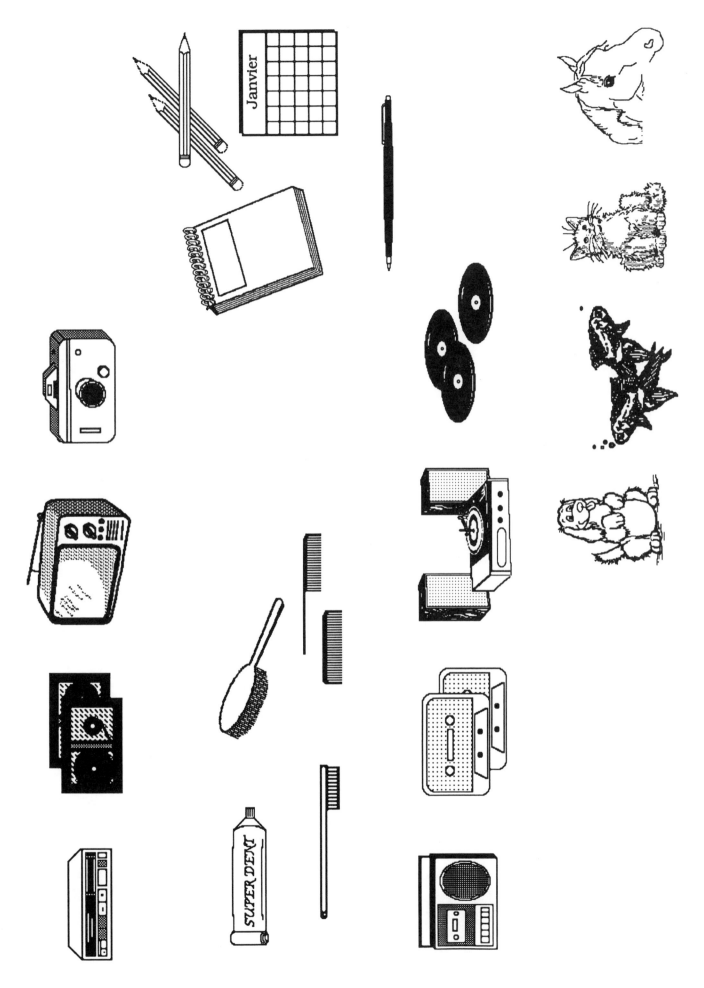

DEUX FAMILLES

A Puzzle and Communication Activity

This activity is adapted from an idea presented by Jan Letson of Fremont High School in Sunnyvale, California, at the Sharing Session of the 1990 CFLTA conference.

Objectives:	*To provide conversational practice and promote effective communication *To reinforce the use of possessive adjectives and of the possessive construction with *de* *To reinforce vocabulary associated with the family
Level:	Advanced beginning or intermediate
Number of students:	Any number of students, working in pairs
Materials:	*One copy of handouts A and B for each pair of students and one copy of the *arbre généalogique* for each student (For the teacher's convenience, page C shows the answers.) *Overhead transparency made from the *arbre généalogique* (optional)
Directions:	*Review appropriate vocabulary and possessive constructions with the class. *One student works from handout A (which has only the vertical words of the crossword puzzle); the other works from handout B (which has only the horizontal). Students may not see each other's papers. *Using the *arbre généalogique* as a reference, students give their partners clues to enable them to fill in their respective versions of the puzzle with the names of the missing family members. (e.g. *Le numéro 5, c'est la fille d'Yves et de Jacqueline Beaupré.* Or: *Tu vois Yves Beaupré? C'est sa fille.*) *At the end of the allotted time period, or when the first pair has successfully completed the activity, the instructor can review the activity by projecting an overhead transparency of the *arbre généalogique* and asking individual students to give sentence clues for each answer.
Note:	The activity works best if the instructor first models the activity, giving clue sentences and having the class guess the answer.

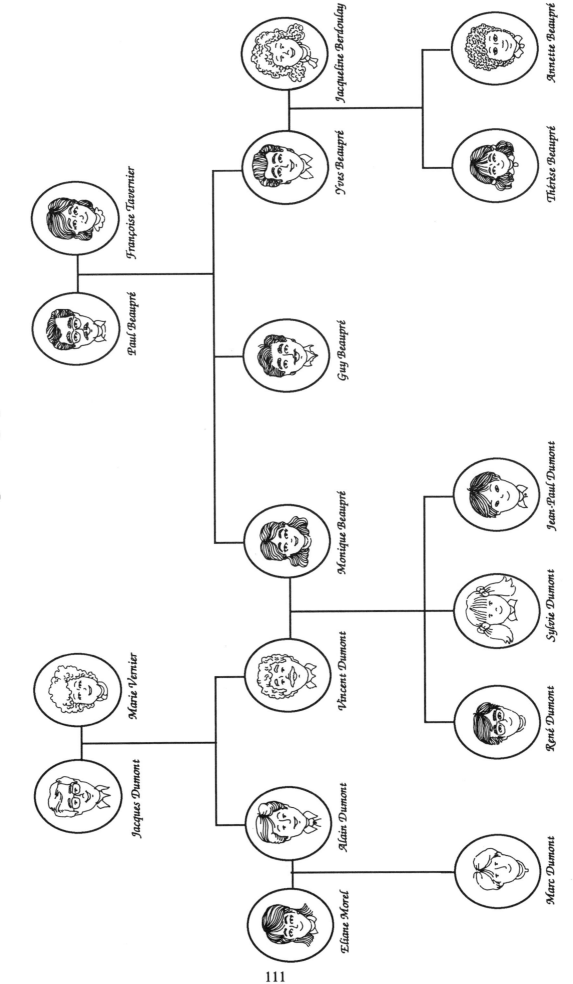

DEUX FAMILLES

un arbre généalogique

Jacqueline Berdoulay

Françoise Tavernier

Paul Beaupré

Yves Beaupré

Guy Beaupré

Annette Beaupré

Thérèse Beaupré

Monique Beaupré

Marie Vernier

Jacques Dumont

Vincent Dumont

Alain Dumont

René Dumont

Sylvie Dumont

Jean-Paul Dumont

Éliane Morel

Marc Dumont

DEUX FAMILLES

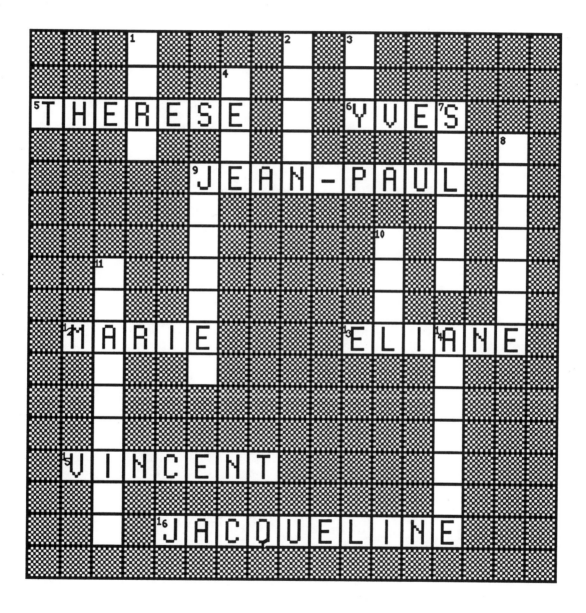

DEUX FAMILLES

			¹M					²A		³G					¹M
			A			⁴R		L		U					
⁵			R			E		A		⁶Y		⁷S			
			C			N		I				Y		⁸M	
					⁹J	E		N				L		O	
					A							V		N	
					C				¹⁰P			I		I	
¹¹F				Q				A			E		Q	
			R	¹²A			U				E		O	
¹²F	R	A	N	C	O	I	S	E		¹³		L	¹⁴A	N	N	E
			N		E		S						N	
			C										N	
			O										E	
¹⁵		I										T	
			S										T	
			E		¹⁶								E	

115

C

DEUX FAMILLES

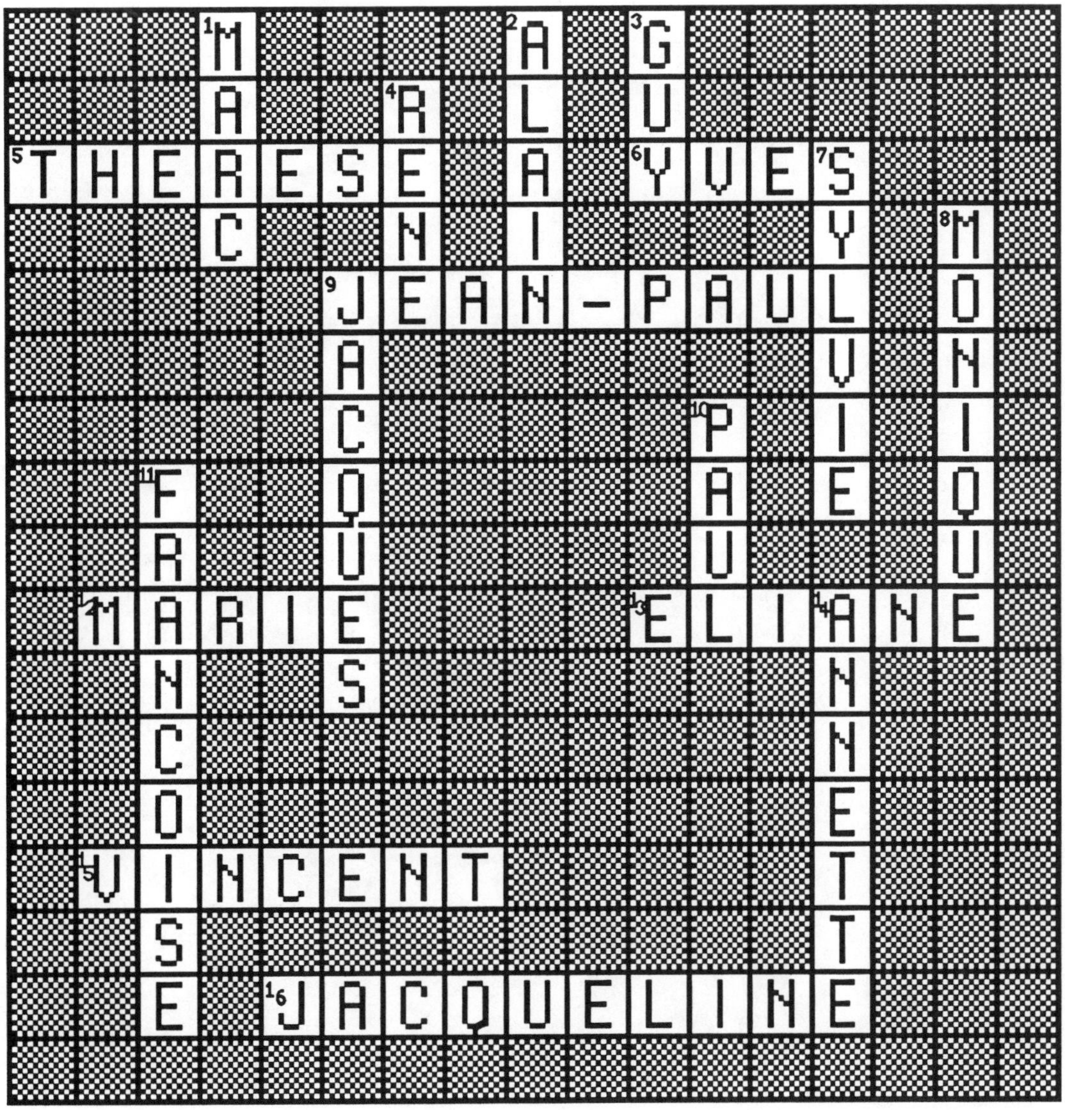
1 MARC
2 ALAIN
3 GUY
4 RENE
5 THERESE
6 YVES
7 SYLVIE
8 MONIQUE
9 JEAN-PAUL
JACQUES
10 PAUL
11 FRANCOISE
12 MARIE
13 ELIANE
14 ANNETTE
15 VINCENT
16 JACQUELINE

LES MAGASINS

A Puzzle and Communication Activity

This activity closely resembles the preceding activity, *Deux familles*. The crossword format can be used to review any set of vocabulary words and can also be used for content material (information about French-speaking countries, French art, literature, history, for example). The software program Crossword Magic (by Mindscape, Inc.), automatically creates crossword puzzles from your own words and will format the clues as well. Be forewarned, however, that the MacIntosh version of the program only works on older versions of the MacIntosh and does not run properly on Mac II's, nor will it print to a Laser Writer printer.

Objectives:	*To provide conversational practice and promote effective communication *To reinforce the vocabulary associated with stores and shopping
Level:	Advanced beginning or intermediate
Number of students:	Any number of students, working in pairs
Materials:	*One copy of handouts A and B for each pair of students *Overhead transparency made from page C (optional)
Directions:	*One student works from handout A (which has only the vertical words of the crossword puzzle); the other works from handout B (which has only the horizontal). Students may not see each other's papers. *Students give their partners clues to enable them to complete their respective versions of the puzzle (i.e. *Un petit magasin où l'on peut acheter des journaux, des revues, des cigarettes ou des timbres = le tabac*). *At the end of the allotted time period, or when the first pair has successfully completed the activity, the instructor can review the activity by projecting an overhead transparency of the answers (page C) and asking individual students to give sentence clues for each answer.
Note:	The activity works best if the instructor first models the activity, giving clue sentences and having the class guess the answer.

Vocabulary used in
activity:

l'alimentation	le marché
la boucherie	le marché aux puces
la boulangerie	la papeterie
la charcuterie	la pâtisserie
l'épicerie	la pharmacie
le grand magasin	la quincaillerie
la librairie	le supermarché

LES MAGASINS

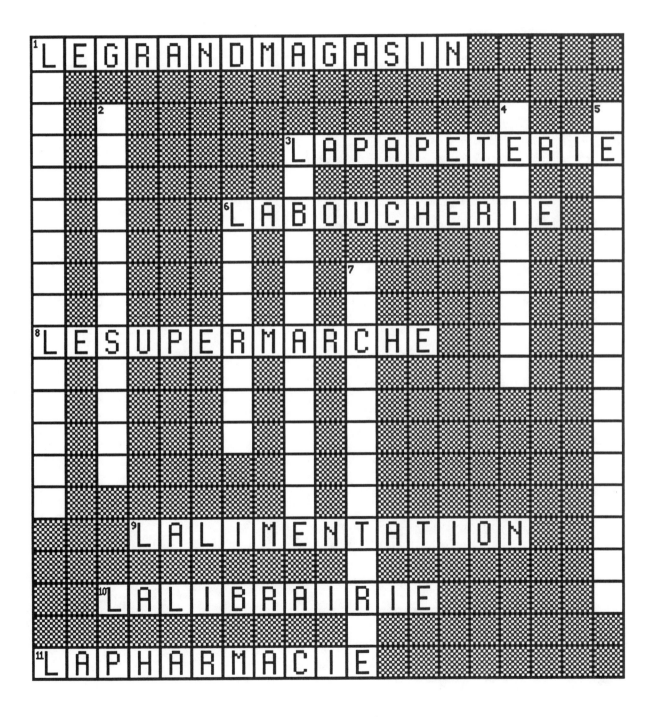

LES MAGASINS

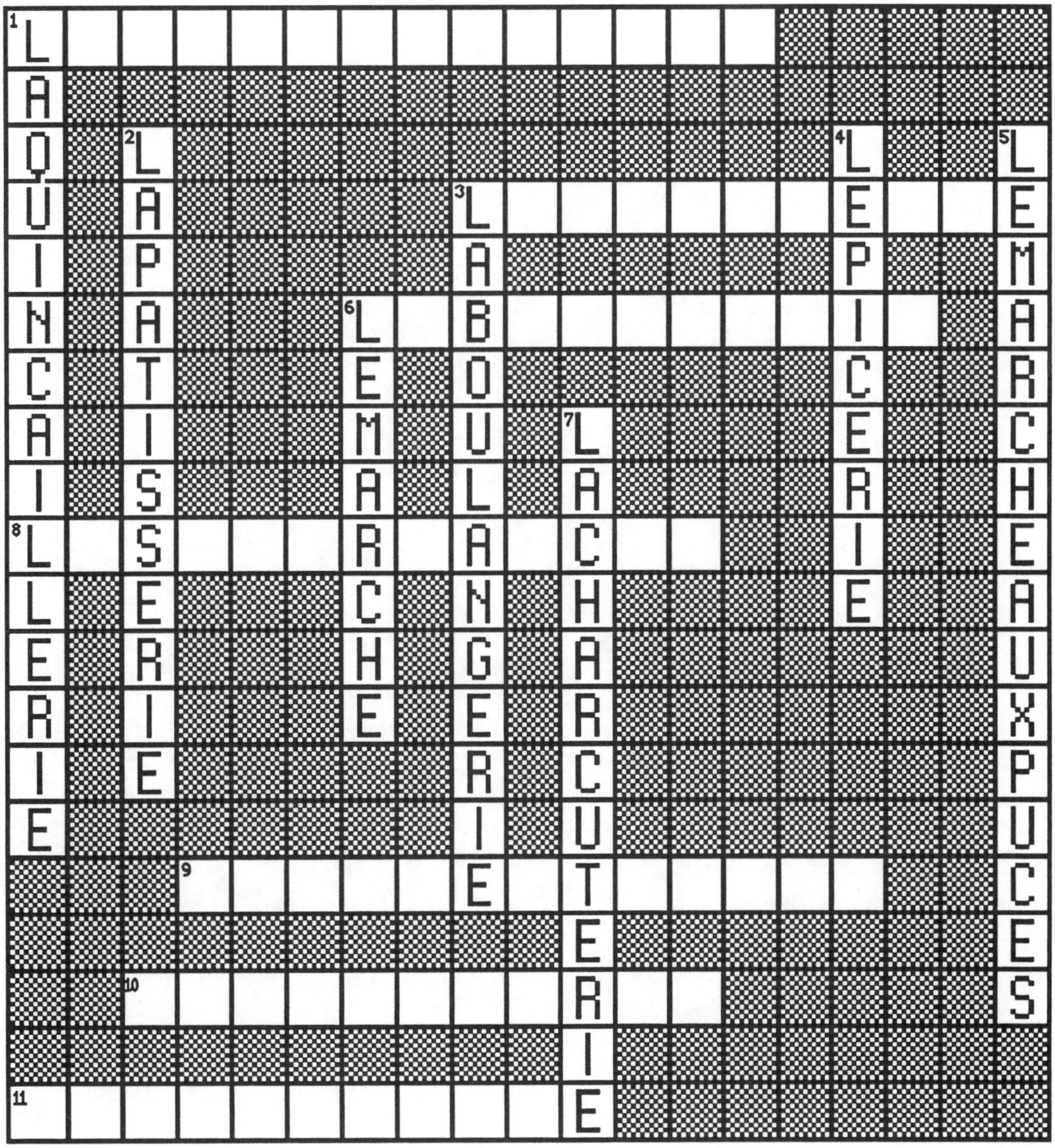
1 LAQUINCAILLERIE
2 LAPATISSERIE
3 LABOULANGERIE
4 LEPICERIE
5 LEMARCHEAUXPUCES
6 LEMARCHE
7 LACHARCUTERIE
8
9
10
11

LES MAGASINS

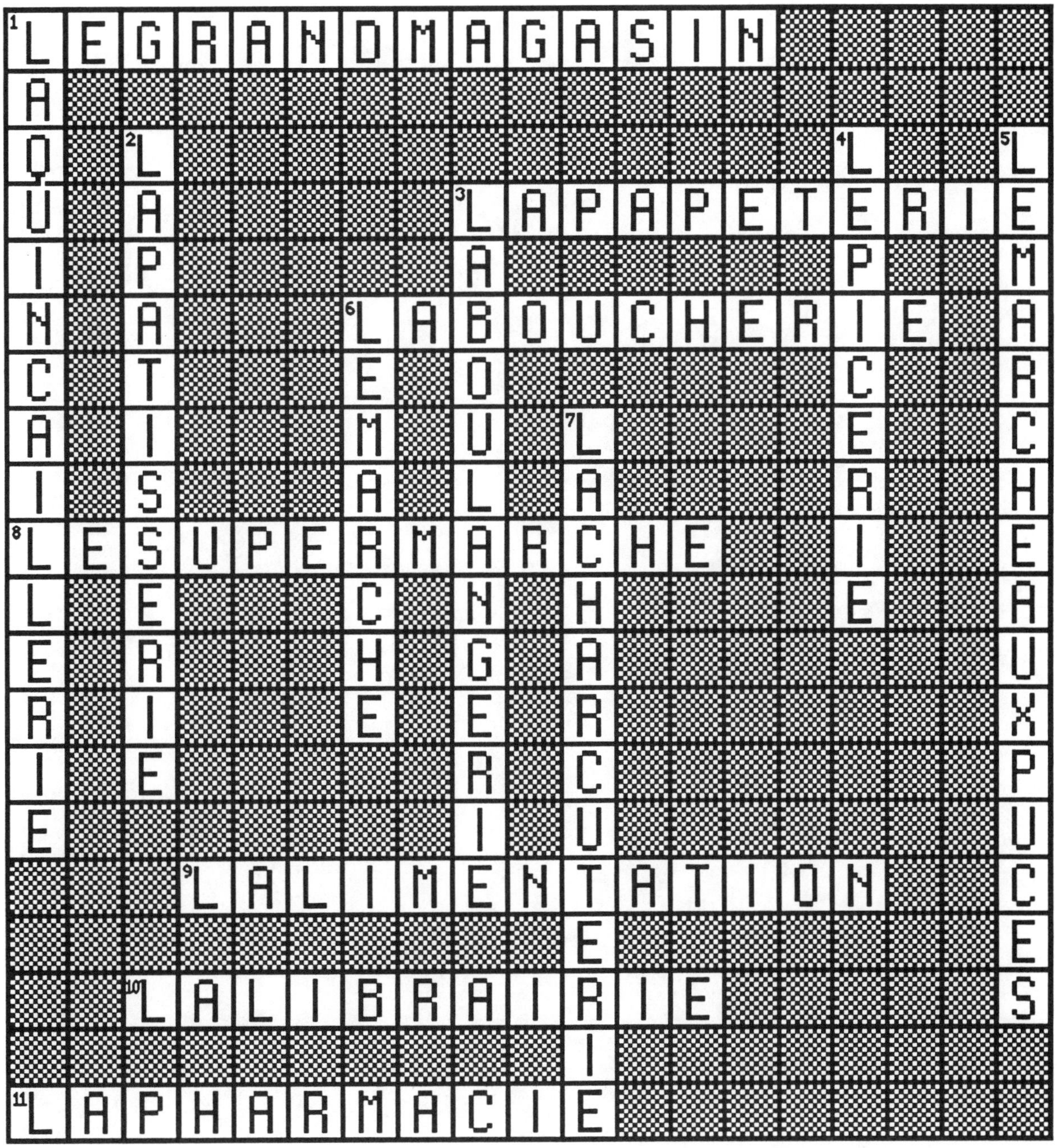
1 LEGRANDMAGASIN
LAQUINCAILLERIE
2 LAPATISSERIE
3 LAPAPETERIE
LABOULANGERIE
4 LEPICERIE
5 LEMARCHEAUXPUCES
6 LABOUCHERIE
LEMARCHE
7 LACHARCUTERIE
8 LESUPERMARCHE
9 LALIMENTATION
10 LALIBRAIRIE
11 LAPHARMACIE

JEU D'IDENTITÉ

A Communication Activity

This exercise can be used at a very early level, as soon as regular -er verbs have been introduced. Vocabulary is minimal and makes use of many cognates. If the various forms of the interrogative have not yet been studied, the exercise can be used to reinforce the interrogative using normal word order and raised intonation.

Objectives:	*To enhance communication skills at an early level *To reinforce the use and conjugation of regular -er verbs *To reinforce the use of the interrogative
Level:	Beginning
Number of students:	Entire class or large group
Materials:	One copy of *Jeu d'identité* fill-in form for each student
Directions:	*After reviewing the conjugation of regular -er verbs and the formation of the interrogative, the class reads over the sentences on the fill-in form together to ensure comprehension and to reinforce correct pronunciation. *Students are then given a designated time to circulate in the classroom, asking questions of their classmates in order to identify a student who fits each description. Students' answers, as well as questions, should be in complete sentence form. Examples should be given of both. In beginning classes, it is important to emphasize that only French will be allowed throughout the activity. *At the end of the time period, the instructor completes the activity by taking a count of how many blanks the students were able to fill in, and then asking different students (who again answer in complete sentences) to identify classmates fitting each description. Follow-up questions can allow further review.
Vocabulary:	The following -er verbs are used in the exercise:

aimer	jouer
détester	manger
écouter	parler
étudier	regarder
habiter	travailler

127

JEU D'IDENTITÉ

Identifiez...

une personne qui écoute souvent la radio _____

un étudiant qui aime la musique classique _____

une étudiante qui déteste la musique classique _____

une étudiante qui parle espagnol _____

un étudiant qui étudie l'informatique _____

une étudiante qui regarde le football à la télé _____

une personne qui habite dans un appartement _____

une étudiante qui mange souvent chez McDonald's _____

un étudiant qui travaille après l'école _____

une personne qui joue du piano _____

JEU D'IDENTITÉ

Identifiez...

une personne qui écoute souvent la radio _____

un étudiant qui aime la musique classique _____

une étudiante qui déteste la musique classique _____

une étudiante qui parle espagnol _____

un étudiant qui étudie l'informatique _____

une étudiante qui regarde le football à la télé _____

une personne qui habite dans un appartement _____

une étudiante qui mange souvent chez McDonald's _____

un étudiant qui travaille après l'école _____

une personne qui joue du piano _____

METTONS LE COUVERT

A Communication Activity

Objectives: *To provide conversational practice and promote effective
                communication
                *To reinforce the use of prepositions
                *To familiarize the student with vocabulary commonly associated
                with table settings and dining rooms

Level: Advanced beginning, intermediate or advanced

Number of students: Any number of students working in pairs

Materials: *One copy of *Mettons le couvert* handout for each pair of students
                *Students will also need an 8 1/2 x 11 blank sheet of paper and a
                pencil

Directions: *One student, working from the handout, describes the dining room
                and set table to his or her partner who is not allowed to see the
                picture.
                *The partner attempts to make an accurate reproduction of the
                drawing by asking questions to confirm the sizes of the various
                objects and their location on the table or in the room.
                *At the end of a stated time period, which will vary according to the
                level of the class, students show their drawings to the class and the
                class votes on which drawing most closely resembles the original.

Notes: *A prize for the winners--and perhaps a booby prize--will liven up
                the competition.
                *Before beginning the activity, a list of prepositions appropriate to
                each class should be reviewed. In beginning classes, the teacher
                may also wish to review the words for items found in the picture.
                *This exercise can also be used to reinforce the use of metric
                measurement if the relative length of a *centimètre* is reviewed
                beforehand and students are encouraged to give approximate
                measurements to help determine location.

DANS DIX ANS

A Writing and Oral Communication Activity

Objectives:
*To provide conversational practice and promote effective communication
*To enhance writing skills
*To reinforce correct conjugation and use of the future tense
*To stimulate a feeling of class camaraderie and allow the students to get to know each other better

Level: Intermediate or advanced

Number of students: May be used by a large group or entire class

Materials:
*Sufficient copies of the first handout so that each student has one writing form (Each handout contains three forms which need to be separated by the teacher.)
*Sufficient number of copies of the second handout (to be completed by the teacher) for the entire class (The number of copies per student will depend on how many writing selections the teacher wishes to include.)

Directions:
*After reviewing the conjugation of the future tense, the class is assigned a short composition (one half to one page in length depending on the level of the class). The topic, *Ce que je serai dans dix ans,* should include how the students imagine their lives will be in ten years--where they will live, their professions, whether or not they will be married, number of children, etc.
*The composition is handed in, corrected by the teacher and returned to the students.
*The students then condense their narratives and copy them over in black ink onto the lined writing form, incorporating any corrections into the condensed version. These forms should be handed in unsigned.
*The teacher collects the shortened versions, pastes them in the boxes on the second handout and makes one copy of each narrative (three narratives are on one page) for each student in the class. If the class is large and/or multiple copies are a problem, the teacher may wish to select a smaller number of narratives for reproduction. Adding a (not too specific) narrative written by the teacher further livens up the activity.
*Students are then given a specified length of time to interview classmates in order to determine the author of each narrative. Questions must be posed in the future tense and answers must be in complete sentences. Examples such as: *Est-ce que tu seras marié(e) dans dix ans?, Combien d'enfants auras-tu?, Où habiteras-tu?* etc. should be given as well as examples of the corresponding answers.

*At the end of the time period, students are surveyed to see how many students they were able to identify and the teacher completes the activity by asking questions, again using the future tense, to identify each student's narrative.

Notes:

*Make sure to allow the students time to read over the narratives before beginning the interview part of the activity. The teacher may wish to read the narratives aloud first or have different students read them aloud. This will reinforce correct pronunciation and give students an opportunity to ask questions about any vocabulary they may not have understood.

*Although this activity may seem somewhat involved at first, the only preparation (aside from the normal correction of writing assignments) is a bit of cut and paste, copying and collating. It provides very effective reinforcement and practice of the future tense in context, both in writing and orally, and is an activity students enjoy. They are very interested in their probable futures and are often very imaginative in their expression of what they feel the future holds for them.

*Dans dix ans...*_____

_____

_____

_____

_____

_____

_____

*Dans dix ans...*_____

_____

_____

_____

_____

_____

_____

*Dans dix ans...*_____

_____

_____

_____

_____

_____

_____

DANS DIX ANS

nom de
l'étudiant(e):

nom de
l'étudiant(e):

nom de
l'étudiant(e):

VOYAGEONS

A Card Game

Like the card game, *Jeu de possessions,* this game is not a true communication activity as it also requires specific, structured responses on the part of the student. It is included here in the hope that it will encourage authentic communication by providing a relaxed, social atmosphere in which to converse, while at the same time reinforcing important, and frequently encountered, basic grammar concepts.

Objectives:	*To reinforce the use of prepositions with geographical names *To emphasize the distinction between commonly used verbs requiring a preposition (with geographical names) and those which don't *To teach the names of well-known countries, cities, provinces, etc. and their locations
Level:	Beginning. Uses two irregular verbs: *aller* and *être* and four common regular verbs: *aimer, travailler, visiter* and *voyager* in the present and near future tenses. Uses the negative and the *est-ce que* form of the interrogative and includes the conditional *je voudrais.* A list of the geographical names used can be found on the following page.
Number of students:	Can be played in pairs or in groups of three or four
Materials:	For each group: *One set of location cards (40 cards containing drawings of countries, provinces, etc.) *One set of cue cards (33 small cards containing partial sentences to be completed by students) Duplicate the location cards "back to back" as shown with answers on reverse side of maps. Cards can be separated using a paper cutter; laminating them first increases their durability.
Directions:	*Location cards are shuffled and placed in a stack with the drawing side up. Cue cards are mixed and placed face down in random order or they can be placed in a box and drawn out one at a time. *The student to the right of the first player holds up the location card from the top of the stack with the drawing facing the player and other students in the group. *The player picks a cue card and reads it aloud, completing the sentence with the appropriate response according to the location card. *Student holding the location card verifies the answer from the correct answers on the back of the card or reads the correct answer if the player's answer is incorrect. One point is awarded to the player for each correct answer. *Play progresses to the student on the left and the procedure is repeated. The student with the most points at the end of the period of play wins.

Note: This game may be adapted to many board games where students
               progress around the board by throwing a die and moving the
               indicated number of spaces for each correct answer. The instructor
               may also assign students to draw maps of France with travel routes
               connecting cities, or world maps with routes connecting
               Francophone countries. These can then be used as as the basis for a
               progressive voyage with students advancing around the map with
               each correct response.

Geographical Names
used in *Voyageons:*   Countries: Cities:

                             l'Algérie   Bordeaux
                             l'Allemagne   Bruxelles
                             l'Angleterre   Londres
                             l'Autriche   Lyon
                             la Belgique   Madrid
                             le Canada   Marseilles
                             la Chine   Montréal
                             l'Espagne   Nice
                             les Etats-Unis   Paris
                             la France   Rome
                             la Hollande   San Francisco
                             l'Italie
                             le Japon
                             le Luxembourg
                             le Maroc
                             le Mexique
                             le Portugal
                             le Sénégal
                             la Suisse
                             le Vietnam

                             Provinces/States: Continents:

                             la Bretagne   l'Afrique
                             la Californie   l'Amérique du Nord
                             la Normandie   l'Amérique du Sud
                             le Québec   l'Europe
                             la Provence

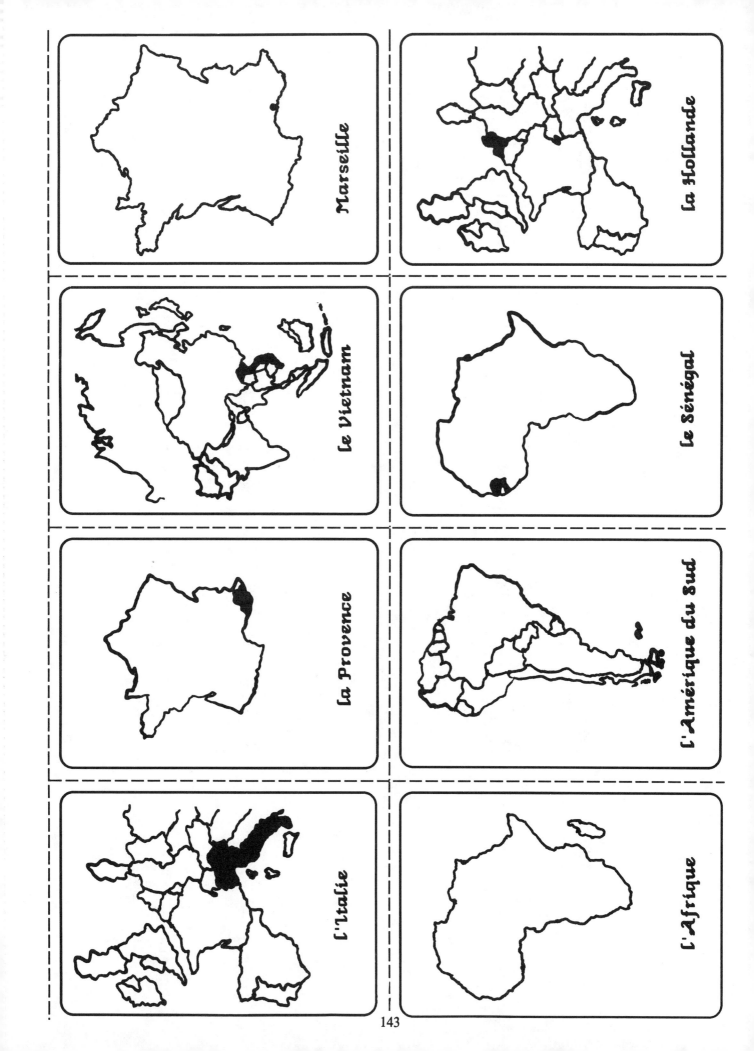

Marseille

la Hollande

Le Vietnam

Le Sénégal

la Provence

l'Amérique du Sud

l'Italie

l'Afrique

143

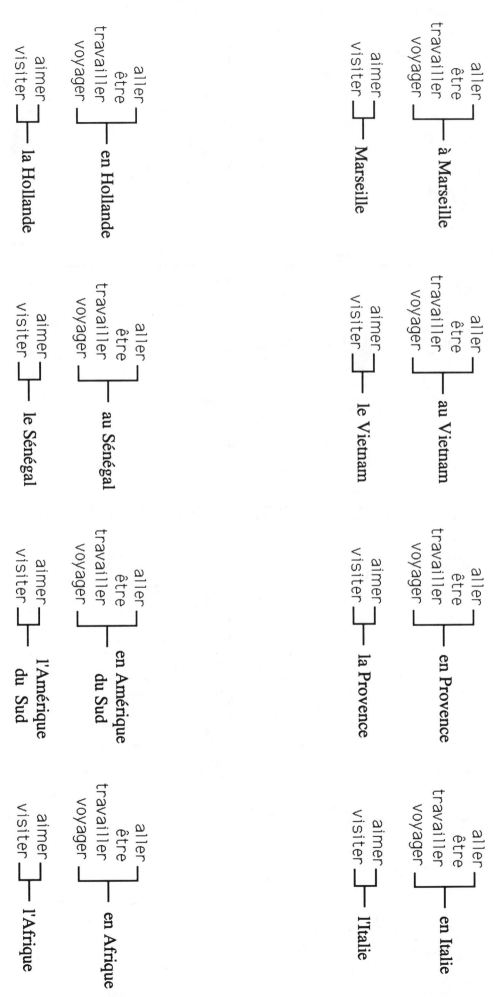

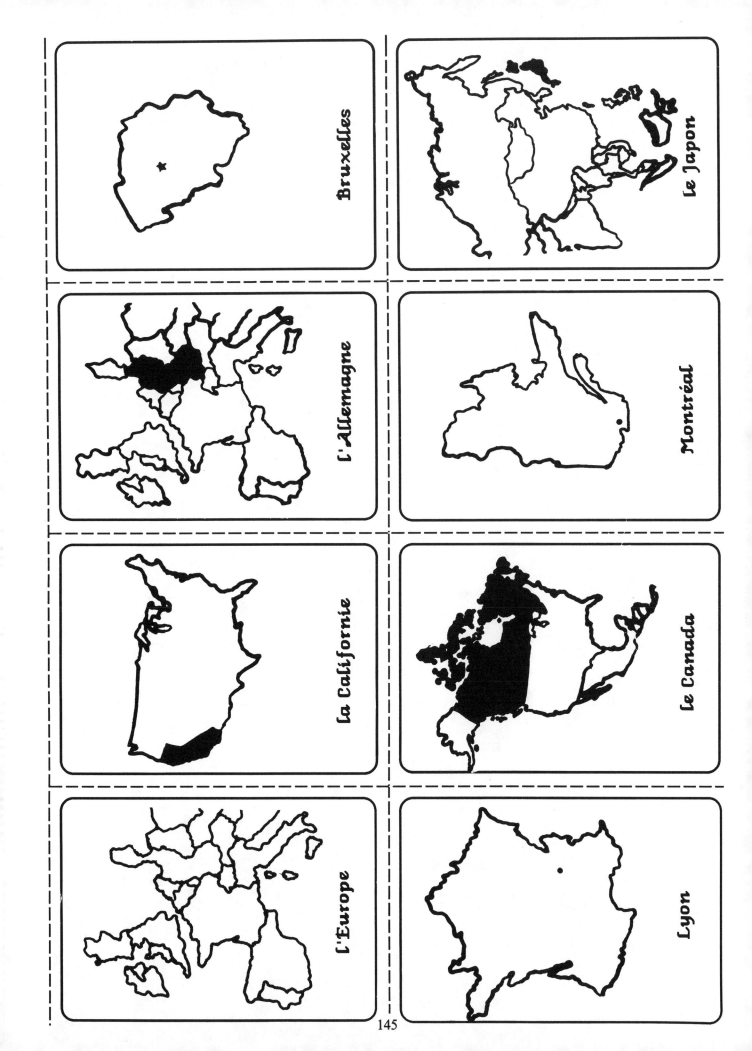

Bruxelles

Le Japon

l'Allemagne

Montréal

la Californie

Le Canada

l'Europe

Lyon

145

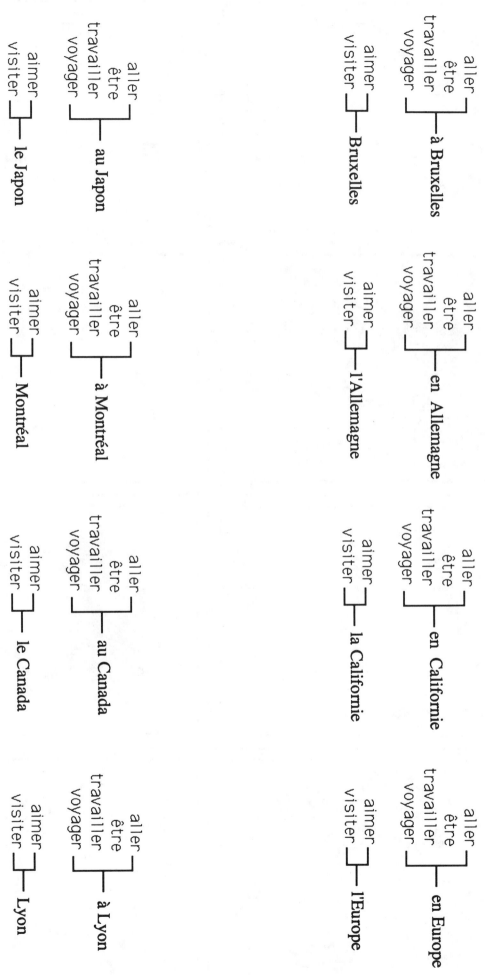

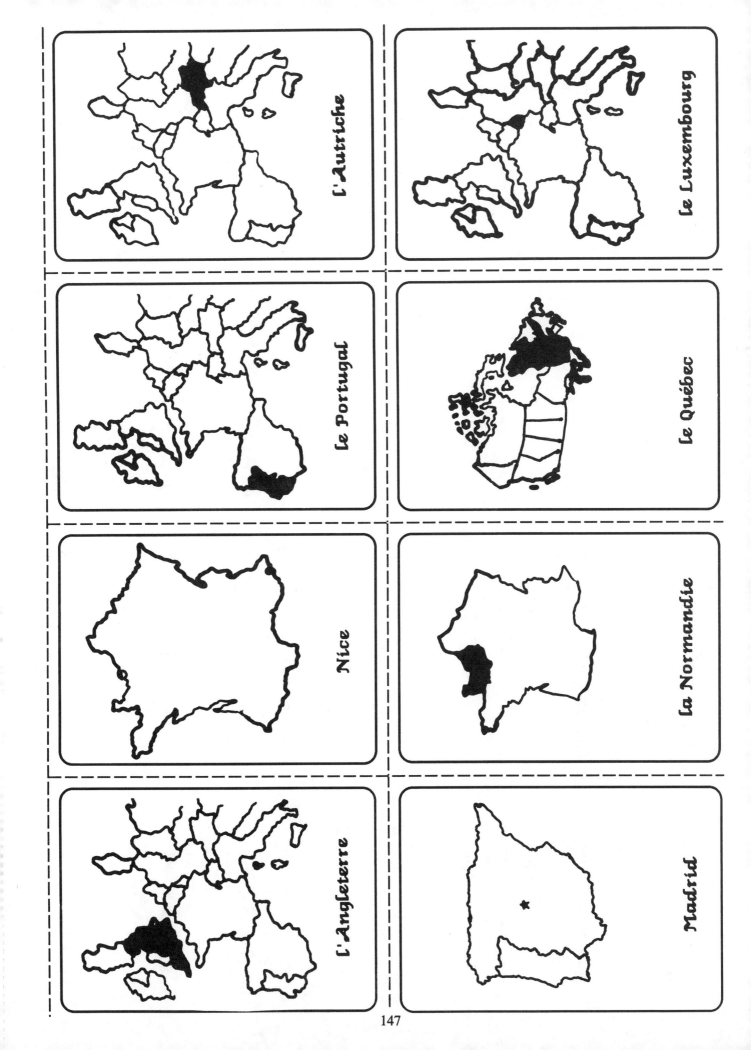

l'Autriche

le Luxembourg

Le Portugal

Le Québec

Nice

la Normandie

l'Angleterre

Madrid

147

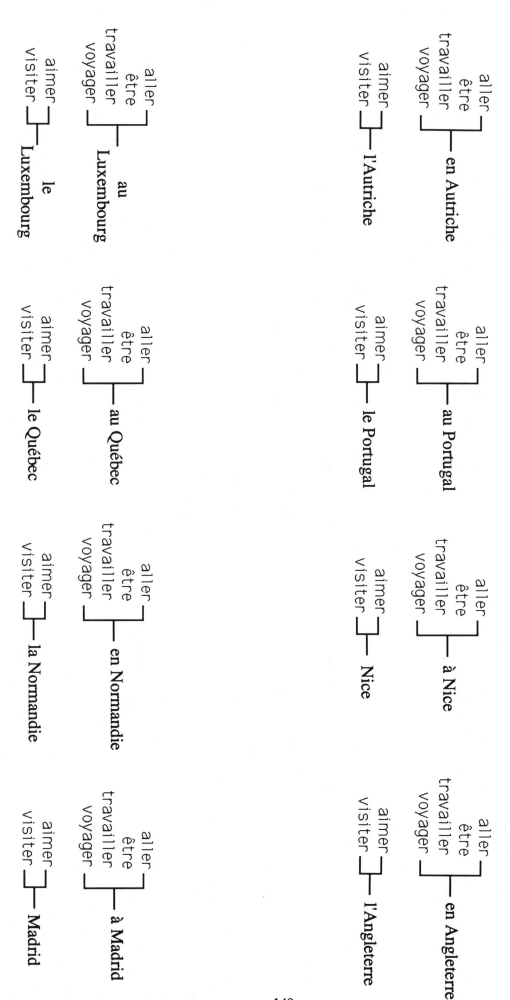

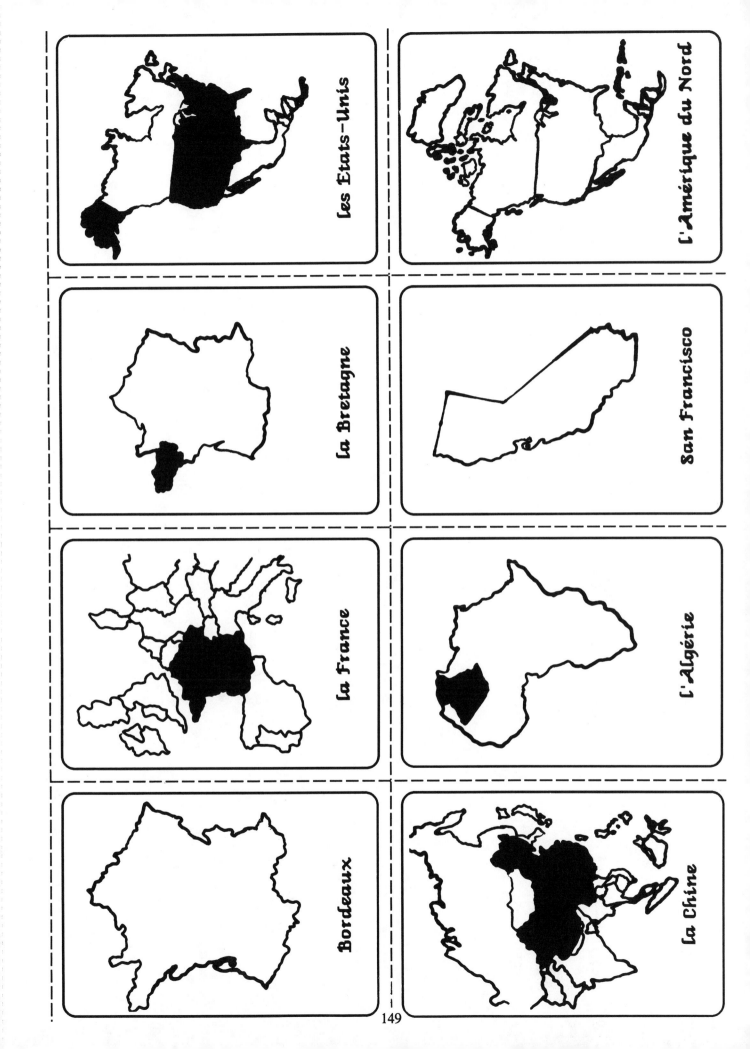

Les États-Unis

l'Amérique du Nord

La Bretagne

San Francisco

la France

l'Algérie

Bordeaux

la Chine

149

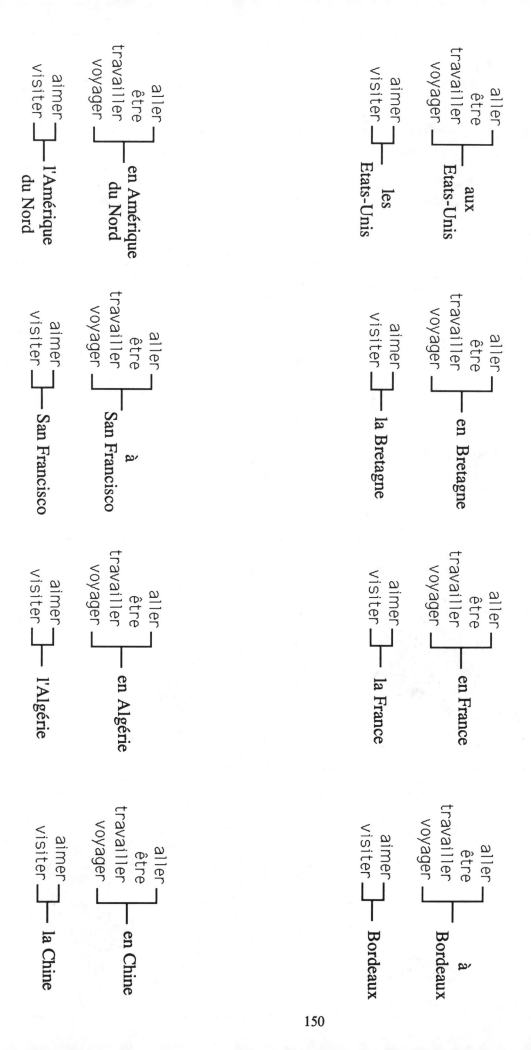

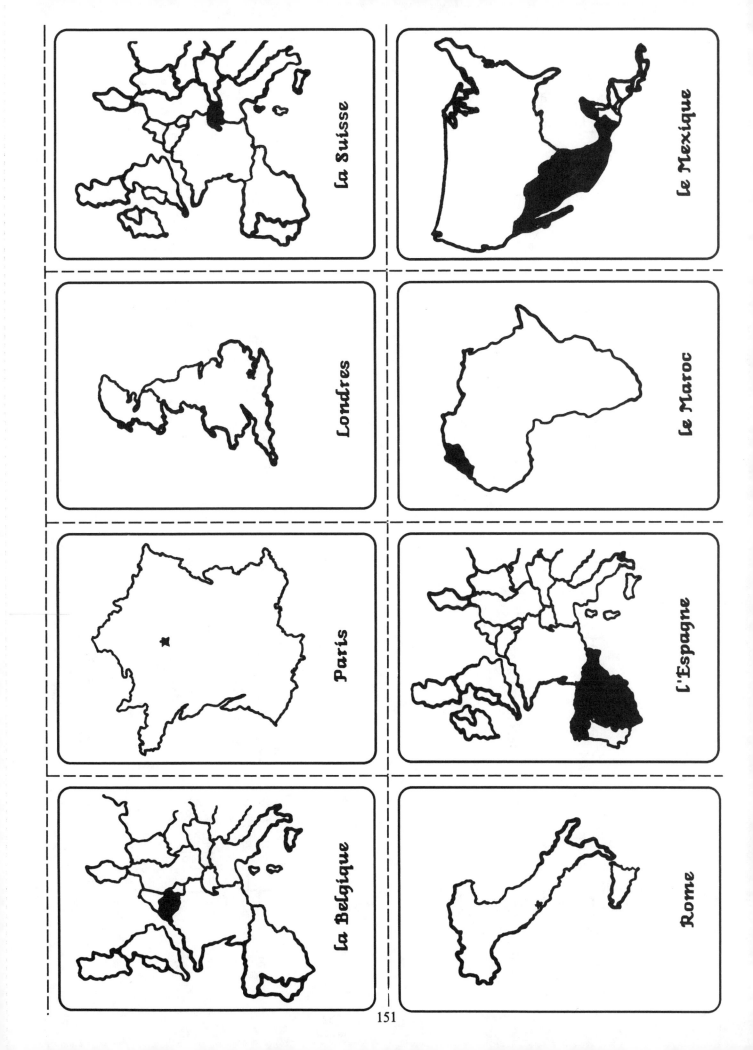

La Suisse

Le Mexique

Londres

Le Maroc

Paris

L'Espagne

La Belgique

Rome

151

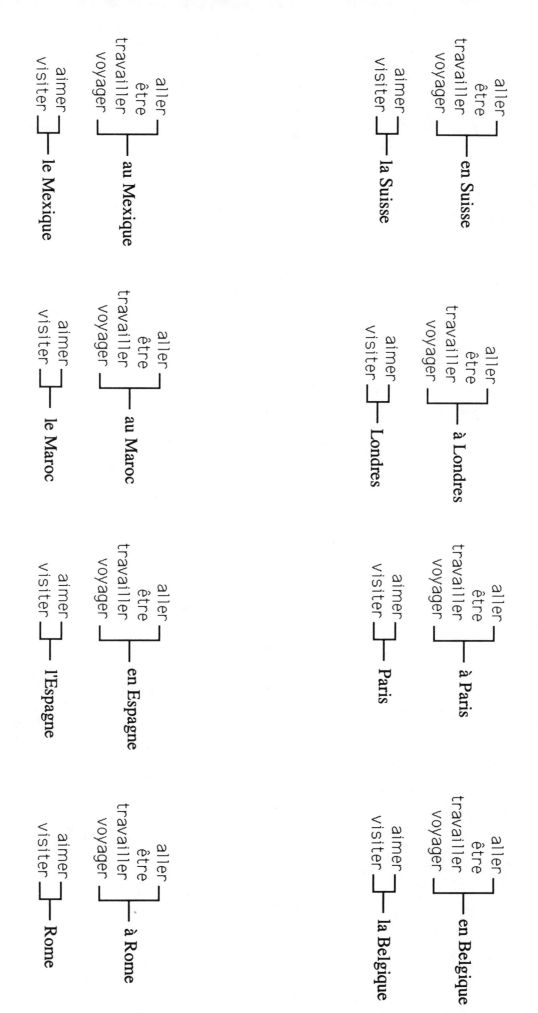

aller
être
travailler
voyager
— en Suisse

aimer
visiter
— la Suisse

aller
être
travailler
voyager
— à Londres

aimer
visiter
— Londres

aller
être
travailler
voyager
— à Paris

aimer
visiter
— Paris

aller
être
travailler
voyager
— en Belgique

aimer
visiter
— la Belgique

aller
être
travailler
voyager
— au Mexique

aimer
visiter
— le Mexique

aller
être
travailler
voyager
— au Maroc

aimer
visiter
— le Maroc

aller
être
travailler
voyager
— en Espagne

aimer
visiter
— l'Espagne

aller
être
travailler
voyager
— à Rome

aimer
visiter
— Rome

152

Je voudrais visiter...	*Est-ce que tu vas visiter...?*	*Nous visitons...*
Nous allons...	*Ils n'aiment pas...*	*Il va...*
Est-ce que tu visites...?	*Je ne vais pas...*	*Je voudrais travailler...*
Est-ce que vous aimez...?	*Est-ce qu'il aime...?*	*Elle est...*
Vous allez visiter...?	*Nous n'allons pas visiter...*	*Ils vont aller...*
Ils vont...	*Je voudrais aller...*	*Elles sont...*
Il n'est pas...	*Nous aimons...*	*Vous allez...?*
Ils travaillent...	*Est-ce que tu vas...?*	*Vous êtes...?*
Nous voyageons...	*Elles vont voyager...*	*Est-ce qu'elle travaille...?*
Elles ne sont pas...	*Est-ce que vous travaillez...?*	*Tu n'es pas...*
Ils visitent...	*On va voyager...*	*Je vais...*

NOUVELLES CONNAISSANCES

A Communication Activity

Objectives: *To provide conversational practice and "break the ice" in a new class at the beginning of a semester
*To facilitate students getting to know each other quickly

Level: Second semester through advanced

Number of students: Entire class or large group

Materials: One copy of *Nouvelles connaissances* handout for each student

Directions: *Students are given a specified length of time to interview at least five different students in French (people they do not already know, if possible) and to list at least three things that they did not previously know about each person. A total time for all five interviews may be specified or the teacher may wish to give about three minutes per individual interview and then announce when each interview period is over.
*When the students have finished, each student is asked to introduce a new student, telling the things he or she discovered during the interview.

Note: If desired, this may be expanded to a writing activity by giving the students time to put answers into complete sentences after the oral part has been done. This could then be handed in to allow the teacher to assess the writing skills of the new class.

NOUVELLES CONNAISSANCES

nom de la personne: renseignements:

1.	a)
	b)
	c)
2.	a)
	b)
	c)
3.	a)
	b)
	c)
4.	a)
	b)
	c)
5.	a)
	b)
	c)

VIVENT LES DIFFÉRENCES

A Communication Activity

Objectives: *To provide conversational practice and promote effective communication
*To reinforce the use of prepositions
*To reinforce the vocabulary commonly associated with the home: rooms, furniture, personal possessions, etc.

Level: Intermediate and advanced

Number of students: Any number of students working in pairs

Materials: *One copy of handouts A and B for each pair
*An overhead transparency of one of the drawings to be used in the review part of the activity (optional)

Directions: *Each partner works with a different version of the drawing. The houses look alike but each room contains differences, some of which are very subtle. There are around 30 differences between the two drawings.
*The object is for the students to determine what the differences are, without looking at each other's drawings. The number of differences should be recorded; students may take notes if they wish.
*At the end of a stated time period, which will vary according to the level of the class, the teacher reviews the activity by first asking how many differences each of the students has found and then by asking individual students to state the differences in specific rooms. An overhead transparency of one of the drawings can be used to facilitate this.

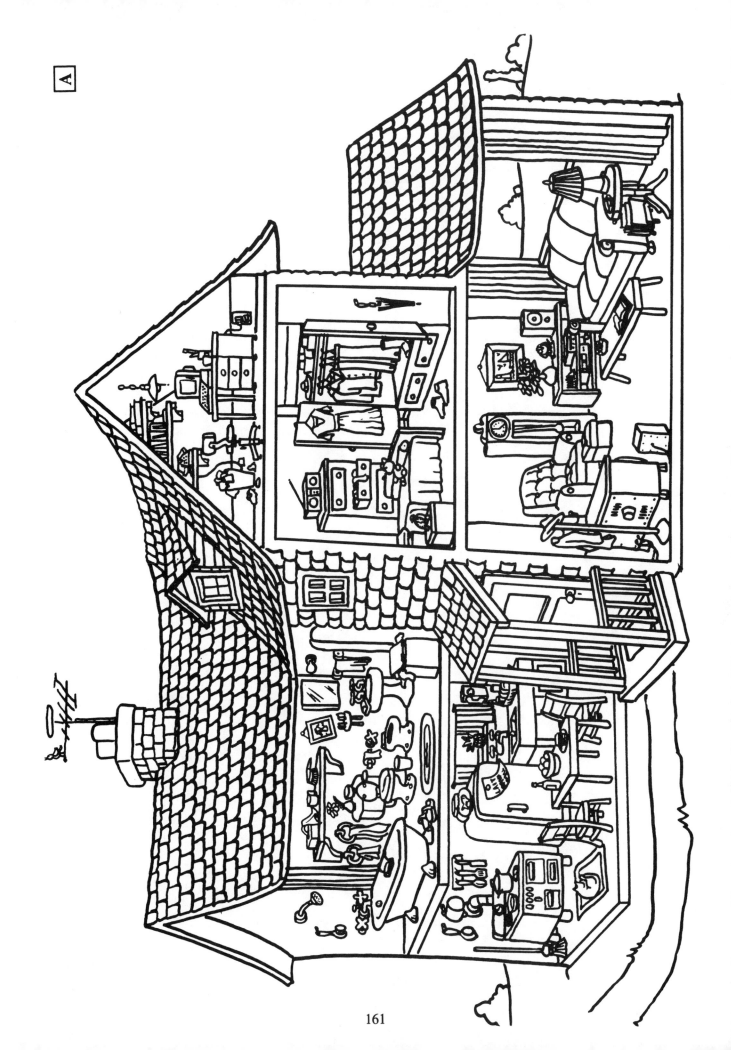

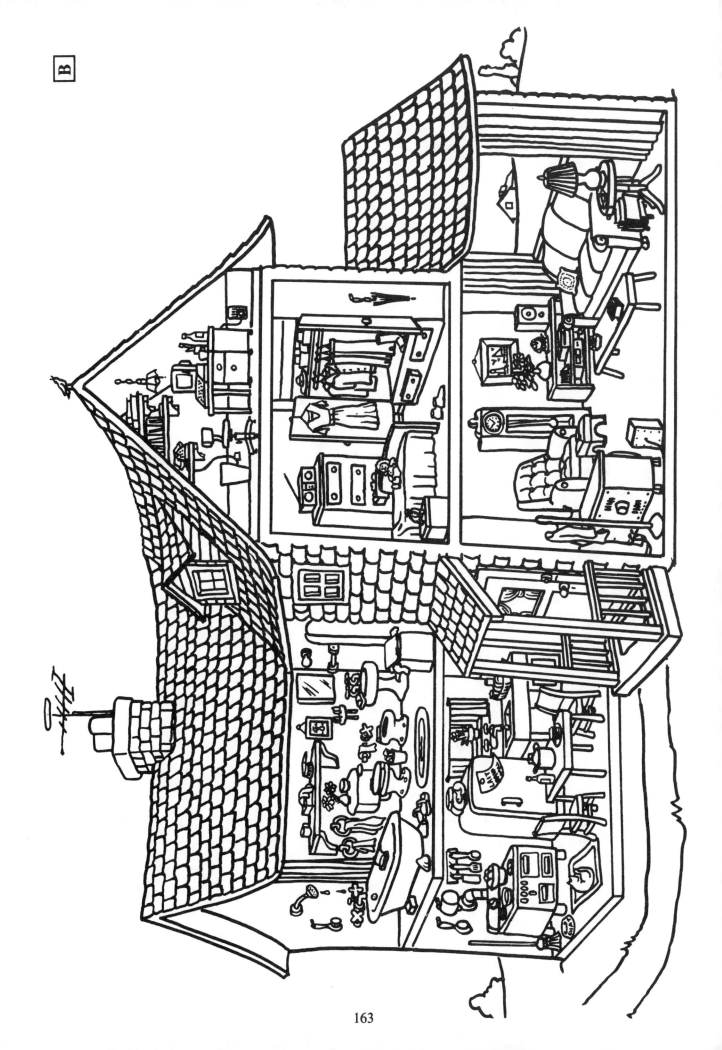

UNE FAMILLE INTÉRESSANTE

A Communication Activity

Objectives:
*To provide conversational practice and promote effective communication
*To stimulate critical thinking
*To reinforce descriptive vocabulary and vocabulary associated with the family
*To practice numbers and the use of dates in context

Level:
Advanced beginning, intermediate or advanced

Number of students:
Groups of two to five

Materials:
*One copy of all four handouts for each group
*One pair of scissors and tape or glue stick for each group

Directions:
*Students construct a hypothetical family, choosing family members from the three pages of photos. For each family member, an identity is constructed complete with name, age, description of character, personality, interests, profession, etc. Short notes can be taken, but the writing of complete sentences is not allowed.
*Each family member's photo is cut out and attached to the *arbre généalogique* and names and dates of birth are written in the spaces provided.
*The group reviews the description of each person and expands the narrative to tell how each of the couples met, what their lives are/were like, etc.
*Depending on the size of the class and the time allowed for the activity, several or all of the groups then present their narratives to the class, illustrating them with the family trees they have constructed.

Notes:
*The time allotted for this activity will vary widely depending on the level of students. The activity is very versatile in that it can be used with different levels and adapted for different grammatical structures. If the class is studying the *passé composé,* for example, all narrative can be given in the past tense. If the class is a beginning class, the descriptions can be very basic and family interactions (requiring more extensive use of verbs) may be omitted. To reinforce numbers and dates, the years of birth and death can be included. Beginning classes may wish to give only the ages of family members.
*This activity can also be used as a basis for a writing assignment with each student preparing a family tree or it can be given as a cooperative writing assignment to small groups.
*As a simpler, quicker version of this activity, students can choose from a collection of pictures of people taken from magazines, etc. and create a single imaginary identity to be presented to the class or to one or two other students working in a group. For this, large full-page photos work best. Students can be asked to bring in photos which can be added to a general collection.

UNE FAMILLE INTÉRESSANTE

arbre généalogique

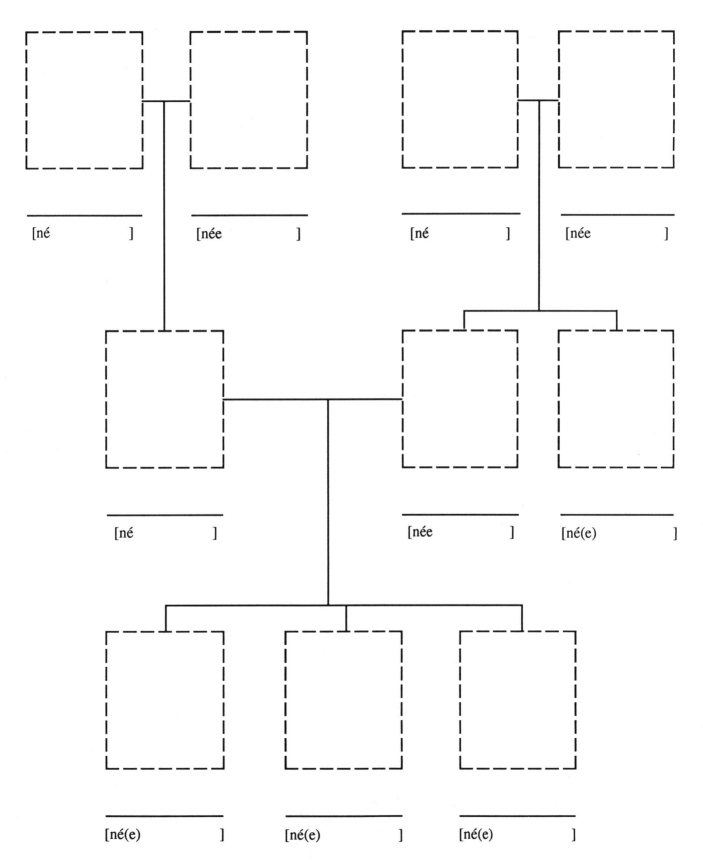

[né   ]   [née   ]   [né   ]   [née   ]

[né   ]   [née   ]   [né(e)   ]

[né(e)   ]   [né(e)   ]   [né(e)   ]

NTC INTERMEDIATE FRENCH-LANGUAGE MATERIALS

Computer Software
French Basic Vocabulary Builder
  on Computer

**Videocassette, Activity Book,
  and Instructor's Manual**
VidéoPasseport—Français

Conversation Books
Conversational French
A vous de parler
Au courant
Tour du monde francophone Series
  Visages du Québec
  Images d'Haïti
  Promenade dans Paris
  Zigzags en France
Getting Started in French
Parlons français

Puzzle and Word Game Books
Easy French Crossword Puzzles
Easy French Word Games
Easy French Grammar Puzzles
Easy French Vocabulary Games
Easy French Culture Puzzles
Easy French Word Games and Puzzles

**Text/Audiocassette Learning
  Packages**
Just Listen 'n Learn French
Just Listen 'n Learn French Plus
Conversational French in 7 Days
Sans Frontières
Practice & Improve Your French
Practice & Improve Your French Plus
How to Pronounce French Correctly

Intermediate Workbooks
Ecrivons mieux!
French Verb Drills

Black-Line and Duplicating Masters
The French Newspaper
The Magazine in French
French Verbs and Vocabulary Bingo
  Games
French Grammar Puzzles
French Culture Puzzles
French Word Games for Beginners
French Crossword Puzzles
French Word Games

Transparencies
Everyday Situations in French

Reference Books
French Verbs and Essentials of Grammar
Nice 'n Easy French Grammar
Guide to French Idioms
Guide to Correspondence in French

Bilingual Dictionaries
NTC's New College French and
  English Dictionary
NTC's Dictionary of *Faux Amis*

For further information or a current catalog, write:
National Textbook Company
a division of *NTC Publishing Group*
4255 West Touhy Avenue
Lincolnwood, Illinois 60646-1975 U.S.A.